DATE DUE

DEC 0 7 2001		
JAN 07 '02		
JUL 29 02		
OCT 14 02		
NOV 11 02		

DEMCO 38-297

window decor

Susan E. Mickey

Sterling Publishing Co., Inc.
New York

Prolific Impressions Production Staff:

Editor: Mickey Baskett
Copy: Sylvia Carroll
Graphics: Dianne Miller, Karen Turpin
Photography: Pat Molnar
Administrative: Jim Baskett
Styling: Susan E. Mickey, Laney McClure

Acknowledgements

Smith+Noble Windoware
Corona, CA 91718
 Mail order source for rods, finials
and brackets. To request Windoware
catalog phone 1-800-765-7776

Plaid Enterprises, Inc
3325 Westech Dr.
Norcross, GA 30092
www.plaidonline.com
 for Gallery Glass paints, Acrylic
 FolkArt paints for decorative painting, stencils, stamps, and block
 printing supplies.

Every effort has been made to insure that the information presented is accurate. Since we have no control over physical conditions, individual skills, or chosen tools and products, the publisher disclaims any liability for injuries, losses, unto-ward results, or any other damages which may result from the use of the information in this book. Thoroughly read the instructions for all products used to complete the projects in this book, paying particular attention to all cautions and warnings shown for that product to ensure their proper and safe use.

Library of Congress Cataloging-in-Publication Data

Mickey, Susan E.
  Window decor / by Susan E. Mickey.
    p. cm.
  ISBN 0-8069-2481-0
    1. Draperies. 2. Windows in interior decoration. I. Title.
  TT390.M53 2000
  645'.3--dc21   00-061895

Published by Sterling Publishing Company, Inc.
387 Park Avenue South, New York, N.Y. 10016
Produced by Prolific Impressions, Inc.
160 South Candler St., Decatur, GA 30030
© 2001 Prolific Impressions, Inc.
Distributed in Canada by Sterling Publishing
c/o Canadian Manda Group, One Atlantic Avenue, Suite 105
Toronto, Ontario, Canada M6K 3E7
Distributed in Great Britain and Europe by Cassell PLC
Wellington House, 125 Strand, London WC2R 0BB, England
Distributed in Australia by Capricorn Link (Australia) Pty. Ltd.
P.O. Box 6651, Baulkham Hills, Business Centre, NSW 2153 Australia

Printed in China
Sterling ISBN 0-8069-2481-0

contents

*The panes of the windows,
all that appears through
them, the going forth in the
morning, the aimless
spending of the day.*

Walt Whitman
Leaves of Grass

This book is a celebration of the window – our "bridge" between inside and outside. There are unlimited ways to decorate the window, from traditional drapes and curtains to blinds and shutters and shades, to window scarves and swags, as well as painted window treatments such as shutters, window boxes, and painted shades. In this book, you'll find a little bit of everything, even some faux stained glass and architectural window treatments, even shades made of branches from your yard. Find your favorite styles and treat your windows as the special features they are.

A simple creative idea can replace yards of fabric with fussy pleats and gathers.

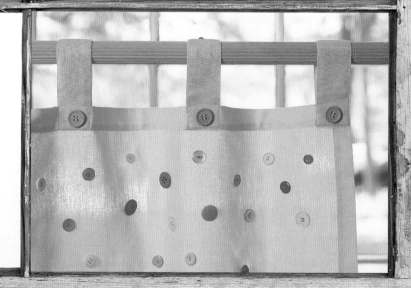

decor

looking out
looking in

Elements of nature can be brought inside to create a window cover that blends the environment with your decor.

We paused to admire the pillared porch; elaborately embossed; The low wide window with their mullions old; The cornice richly fretted, of grey stone; and that smooth slope from which the dwelling rose.

William Wordsworth

Pick a style for a special room or choose a style for your whole environment.

styles
for
your
windows

Your style will have its
own voice.

Your style will frame
your world.

Always choose the style of window decor before buying your fabric and trim. Falling in love with a piece of fabric or a certain finial, then trying to make it fit your house, will certainly cause unnecessary frustration. Consider these simple things as you spend your time dreaming and planning your window treatments.

• How much time will I spend looking at this window? Will it be something I want to change every few years, or seasonally? If the answer is "yes," then think about a style that will be easy to recreate with new fabrics or a coat of paint.

• Is this window treatment for decoration or privacy? The answer may be BOTH, but if you are trying to reduce the visibility from the outside world, consider a style that covers the window completely at times.

• How formal or informal is my lifestyle? Will I be entertaining a great deal in this room and have people moving about? If this is the case, consider a style that can change as the sun goes down or as candles are lit, by pulling back a part of the drape or pulling down a shade. Also consider a style that can be informally tied up or pulled out of the way of feet and playing children.

• What colors are currently in my home, and what colors would I like to embrace with this window decor? Consider enhancing the existing colors in your rooms or use your windows to add a highlight of color that does not currently exist in your environment.

Consider the following styles and colors while you are planning your windows.

traditional
ideas

This style embraces antique furniture and classic designs. Fabrics used have lots of texture – brocades, heavy cottons, velvets. There is usually a distinct presence of surface design, with porcelain textures being mimicked on the fabric designs. Subtle colors can mix with jewel tones for this familiar room.

colors: Plum • Mauve • Tobacco • Gray

contemporary ideas

Elements of this style include clean lines, smooth surfaces, subtle textures, and a lack of surface details. Color palettes can be neutral and narrow or may embrace vivid and vibrant spectrums.

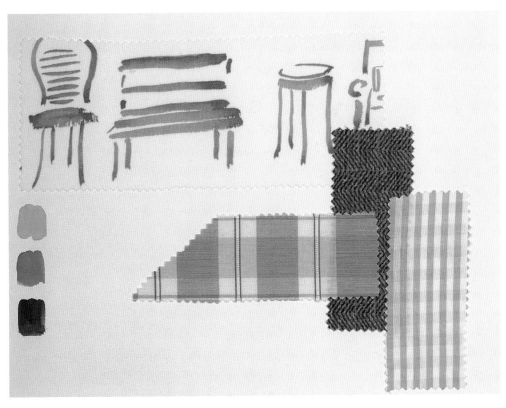

colors:

- Granny Smith Green
- Yellow
- White
- Olive

This style is characterized by primitive antiques and traditional color palettes. It is a great way to use the family heirlooms and flea market finds that are less formal and more user friendly.

country ideas

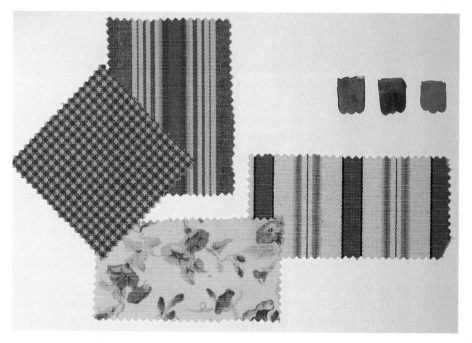

colors:

- Rooster Red
- Barnwood
- Brown
- Dark Mossy Green

cabin casual ideas

Heavy texture and rustic furniture go hand in hand with the earth tones and colors of nature that define this style.

colors:
- Fall Leaf Gold • Brown
- Woodsy Green • Earth Red

whimsical ideas

A colorful and eccentric touch is needed for this fanciful style. Bright, vibrant colors accentuate this look.

colors: Orange • Blue • Green

There are certainly many choices of rods available today. Here are some readily available styles as well as make-your-own project ideas. All a rod needs to be is sturdy, durable, and pleasing to look at. Brackets can also be made of any number of household items and found objects.

rods,
hardware
& trims

wooden rods

Hardware stores carry a variety of dowels and rods that can be cut to a specific length for your window needs. They can be smooth or fluted, finished or unfinished. You can finish them yourself with stain or a bright paint color. These rods will need a finial on each end to finish the look. Find a bracket to hold the rod that matches the style of rod and finial that you have created. Or, you can attach elbow joints to the ends of the rods so that they can be attached to the wall.

There is a great variety of hardware on the market from which to choose for hanging your curtains and drapery. Use your imagination and your own style to combine components to make the hardware that is right for your window. You make your rods and buy finials and brackets to match or vice versa. Mix metal and wood or use natural elements with metal. Here are some ideas to get you started.

pvc rods

PVC pipe is readily available at hardware stores and can be found in a variety of widths. It is inexpensive and can be used as a substitute for wood or metal poles. However, use PVC only if it will be covered with the fabric pocket. Finials can be fitted to the end of the pipe. PVC elbows are also available to attach to the ends of the poles and then the elbows are mounted to the wall beside the window.

choose a rod & hardware

metal poles

Most hardware stores or drapery departments have metal poles to use for curtain hanging. They are available in a variety of diameters, lengths in finishes — such as wrought iron, brass, and silver. They also come in many styles, including smooth, twisted, and fluted. Some have finials already attached, others have a choice of finials that can be attached to the ends.

spring rods

These tension rods can fit inside the window frame and avoid any holes or screws in the woodwork. They will work best for lightweight fabrics and materials.

metal brackets

Metal finishes have become popular in recent years. They can be purchased at any home decor or do-it-yourself home supply store. They are also available in many catalogs.

wooden brackets

They come in many finished and unfinished surfaces. They can be finished the same as the rod, or even in a contrasting finish. They can be used with or without rods, as shown in the "Simple Window Scarf" project. They are easy to install and can add the finishing touch to your window treatment.

choose a bracket

rings & hooks

This type of hardware can help you hang anything easily. Classic rings slide over the rod and a drapery hook fits into the eye screw. Cafe rings attach directly to any fabric or material and give a little more distance between the rod and the fabric. Grommets can be installed in fabrics and are an interesting detail. They come in all sizes and can be used by themselves or combined with rings for hanging.

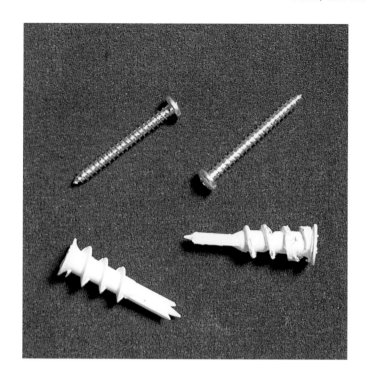

Install your brackets before any other part of your window treatment project. Brackets can be hung 1) on the woodwork of your window; 2) on the wall beside the window; or 3) above the window between the window frame and the ceiling. Large brackets are usually installed 2" outside the window frame so that there is not too much space between the curtains and the window. If you are installing into wallboard or plaster, you will need to secure your brackets with an anchor or a bolt. Here are some easy installation tips for you to use.

supplies

Plastic anchors or toggles
Bolts
Drill
Screwdriver
Pencil
Measuring tool

installing hardware

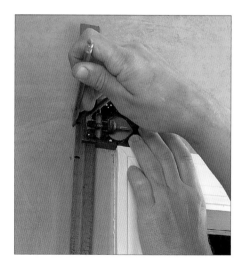

1 Mark the wall beside the window.

2 Drill holes for the plastic anchors or toggles. Use a drill bit that is slightly smaller than the diameter of the plastic anchor or toggle.

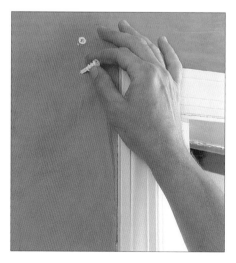

3 Insert the plastic anchors or toggles into the drilled holes and tap in with a hammer.

4 Place the hardware and insert the screw through the hardware. Attach into the plastic anchor or toggle.

Measuring your window correctly is the most important part of any successful window project. Take your time to do this step thoroughly. A correct measurement will ensure an easy installation.

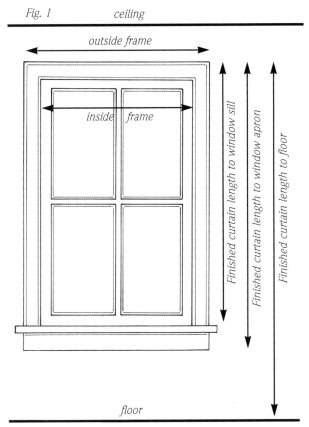

Fig. 1
ceiling
outside frame
inside frame
Finished curtain length to window sill
Finished curtain length to window apron
Finished curtain length to floor
floor

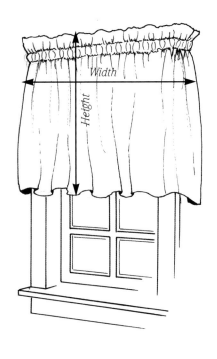

Fig. 2
Outside Mount
Width
Height

measure your windows

Fig. 3
Inside Mount
Width
Height

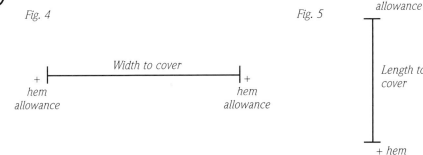

Fig. 4
Width to cover
+ hem allowance
+ hem allowance

Fig. 5
+ hem allowance
Length to cover
+ hem allowance

how to measure

1. Use a metal retractable tape measure to take the most accurate measurements. If you don't have a tape measure, use a wooden yardstick. Take the measurements needed as shown on Fig. 1. Make a drawing of your window and write in these measurements. Once you have all these necessary measurements, you can determine how much fabric you need, depending upon the window treatment you choose.

2. Select an inside or outside mount for your window treatment:
See Fig. 2 showing an outside mount. An outside mount is the most common mount for curtains and drapery. The hardware for this kind of mount may be secured on the window frame or on the wall outside the frame. If there are center support brackets needed and you are going to mount the side brackets on the wall, be sure they are high enough so that the center support will clear the top of the frame. An outside mount will make your window appear larger, it can hide an unsightly window frame, and when the curtain is open, will provide a more open view.

See Fig. 3. showing an inside mount. For an inside mount, be sure that the frame is deep enough to accommodated the depth of the window treatment with its hardware so that the treatment is flush with the front of the frame. Blinds, roller shades, and curtains on spring rods most often use an inside mount. An inside mount is best for some treatments because it provides a finished, built-in look without covering your window molding.

Options for how high to mount curtain rods:
• Mount up to the ceiling.
• Mount centered between the top of the window frame and the ceiling.
• Mount even with the top of the window.
• Mount inside the window.
• Mount 1"-2" above the window frame.

Options for width mounting of curtain rods:
• Mount even with the outside edge of the window frame.
• Mount 1" - 2" from the outside edge of window frame.
• Consider what is beside the windows (cabinets, corners, etc.) and determine mounts accordingly.

Window Measuring Tips:
• Another useful way to measure your window is to use a ribbon or string cut to the finished length of your curtain or window treatment. You can then measure the ribbon at the fabric store with a ruler.
• Draw your window on a piece of graph paper. Be sure to include the ceiling and the floor so that you can get an idea of the scale of your design. This will help you get accurate measurements of fabric.
• Install the hardware on your window and retake the measurements for your curtains. Record your measurements on your sketch. Remember to include in your sketch the amount the fabric may hang down from a ring or hook on the curtain rod.
• You may install your window decor inside the frame, on the frame, or outside the window frame on the wall.
• If you are hanging your rods on large brackets that will be placed on the wall outside the window frame, most brackets are placed about 2" outside the frame and about 2" above the frame. Allow for this in your measurements.
• Always remember to allow for things that may interfere with your installation, like kitchen cabinets, close corners, or architectural detail.

Fig. 6

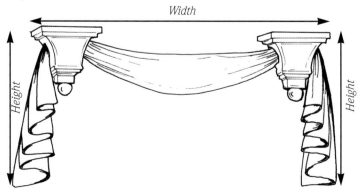

fabric
measurements
for panels:
1. Determine the width and length of the area you wish to cover. Mark down these measurements.
2. Add the hem allowances to all measurements.
3. If you want fullness in your curtains for a gathered window treatment, double the measurement width. Divide this by the number of fabric panels you will have on the window. Usually you will need two panels. For sheer or thin fabrics, you may use 2-1/2 or 3 times the finished width measurement.

for scarves and swags:
Scarves and swags can be mounted through rings, sconces, tiebacks, or simply draped over a rod. Scarves look great in many different lengths – framing a window, half-way down a window, to the floor, or even puddled on the floor. To determine the length of fabric needed, see Fig. 6 and follow the instructions below:
1. Measure the width of the window area you wish to cover.
2. Measure the length down each side for the fabric drop.
3. Add the width, plus the length of each side.
4. Add a hem allowance for each end of the fabric.

Fabric Measuring Tips
• If you have a repeating pattern to match, add more yardage to accommodate the pattern.
• Remember to allow for tall ruffles or headers on the top of your curtain or window treatment. Determine if you want these above the window frame or flush with the window frame at the top. Hang your hardware accordingly.
• Working with a friend or helper is recommended. Have someone hold the fabric or treatment up to the window while you stand away and look with an objective eye.
• When measuring for fabric, round your measurements down to the nearest 1/2". Small fractions of an inch will be noticeable for most curtains or drapery treatments.

ribbons, cords, and tassels

Ready made cords and tassels can be found in drapery departments and cut to measure. Ribbon can also make wonderful tie backs.

tie backs & trims

clothespin keepsakes *designed by Laney McClure*

Here are some clever ideas for decorations that can be fastened to a curtain or that can be used as a tie back. Here we used a wooden clip clothespin, but anything that will clip onto a rod or slide on a wire can hold your window decor.

supplies

Plain wooden clothespins
Various decorative attachments (silk flowers, glass beads, wooden cutouts, clear picture frames, or other desired items)
Hot glue sticks and glue gun

instructions

1. Prepare decorative attachments.
2. Attach decorations to clothespins with hot glue.
3. Use clothespins to hold curtain fabric to curtain hardware such as wire or small rods.

floral tie backs
designed by Laney McClure

supplies

Various silk flowers

Wire cutters

Wall screw, 3"

Wire edged ribbon, 2" wide

Floral tape

instructions

1. Trim stems of silk flowers with wire cutters, leaving a 2" stem on each.
2. Bundle the flowers and secure all the stem ends together with floral tape.
3. Cut a length of ribbon long enough to go around the body of the curtain. Tie both ends to the back of the floral bundle, creating a loop for the curtain to fit through.
4. Attach screw to wall at the appropriate height and attach floral bundle to it, using the exposed stems as an anchor.∽

metal hardware tie back

Simply attach tie back to the wall, pull back the curtain, and place it in the tie back.

natural tie back
designed by Susan E. Mickey

supplies

Vine from a deconstructed vine wreath

Grape cluster

Dried straw tassels

Variegated ribbon

Floral wire

instructions

1. Weave the vines together.
2. With floral wire, attach the grapes on the vine.
3. Tie straw tassels around the vine.
4. Tie ribbon onto vine.
5. Secure all to a hook on your window frame or wall.

Fabric is the most popular of all materials for decorating windows. It is versatile and it softens the overall decor. Fabric can be turned into drapes, curtains of all styles, swags, window scarves, and valences. Fabric can cover cornices. Fabric can hang freely or be tied back or held firmly in a precise place by gathering it on a rod at the top and the bottom. It can be gathered or used as ungathered panels. It can be made into tabs that take the place of rings.

Fabric can also be stamped or block printed with paint for further decoration. It can even be glued (with iron-on webbing) to avoid sewing, if desired.

In addition, there are almost unlimited colors, prints, and textures to choose from to perfectly satisfy your preferences. Window treatments will set the tone of your room.

fabric
window decor

When making your own window treatments, there are a few basic techniques that will help you with a successful project. If you are already skilled on a sewing machine, these will be almost self explanatory. If you are a beginning stitcher, do not be afraid – these techniques are easy and should not cause stress. If you do not stitch at all, we will suggest some non-sewing alternatives to help you achieve a finished project. Most important is the ability to take your time and do each step thoroughly. This will help you enjoy the process and achieve more satisfying results.

Lining your curtains is a matter for effect. Sheers or thick silks should not be lined because the effect you wish to achieve is having light come through the curtains. Thin cottons and chintz look better lined and are much more durable and fade resistant if a lining is added. Lining adds body, and may even be used for energy efficiency. Also, if a curtain is to be viewed from the outside, a lining will help to cover the back, hiding seams, hems, or the unprinted side of the fabric.

finishing techniques
working with fabric

Before cutting your fabric and lining. Preshrink it by ironing it with a steam iron. Have your ironing board and iron beside the area where you are sewing. Pressing is very important to insure a professional look. Pressing each seam as you work is one of the most important things you can do to ensure a finished and clean look.

finished edges

hems

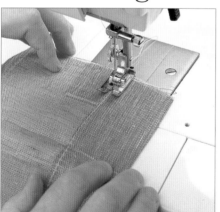

To finish the sides of your curtain, fold the edge over and press well. Fold down 1-1/2" and press again. Sew next to the fabric edge either on the machine or by hand.

Fold up the bottom edge of the fabric 3" and press. Fold again 3" and press. Hand stitch or machine stitch the hem in place, stitching at the top edge of the fabric fold.

Non-Sewing Alternative: You can do the previous steps by ironing on fusible webbing or other heat-and-bond fusible fabric product.

layered tabs

This effect is achieved by layering two curtains. The green tab curtain in the photo is bottom layer, and was purchased with the pre-sewn tabs. The top layer is a gauze curtain tied to the rod with 12" lengths of sheer ribbon. The top layer is dropped below the bottom layer.

tabs for curtain tops

silk tied strips

Each silk strip is 3" wide and has a zigzag finish on each edge. The strips are tied with a slip knot over the rod.

how to make sewn tabs

To make tabs for the tops of the curtains, follow these easy instructions. You can make your tabs out of contrasting fabric or matching fabric. You can edge them with piping or trim, and decorate them with buttons or accessories.

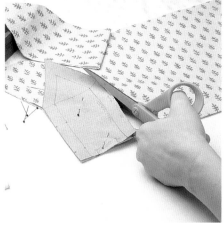

1 Cut double the number of tabs needed, following the tab pattern.

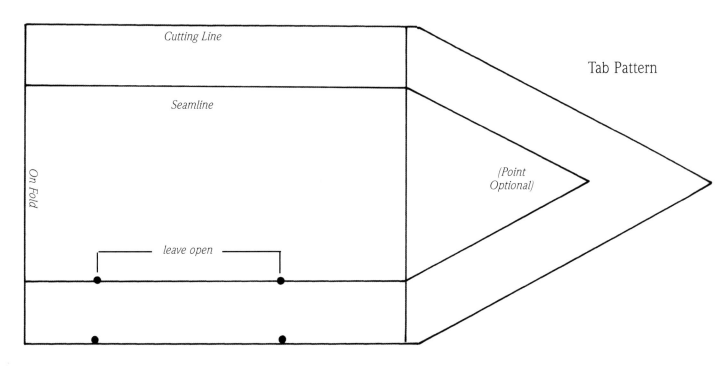

Cutting Line

Tab Pattern

Seamline

On Fold

(Point Optional)

leave open

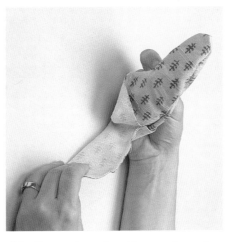

2 Put two tabs right sides together and stitch around the outside on the stitching lines. Leave the space between the dots unsewn to have an opening for turning.

3 Turn tabs right side out through unsewn opening.

4 Press tab and hand sew opening shut. Or topstich the tab all the way around on the machine.

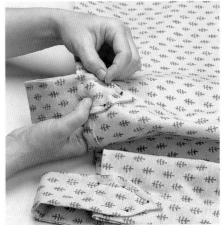

5 Pin the tab in place at top of finished curtain, pinning through the curtain and aligning the back of the tab with the front of the tab.

tied tabs
These tabs are made with extra length so they can be tied over a spring rod.

6 Stitch the tabs to the top of the finished curtain. ∾

simple
window scarf

This is the simplest kind of window treatment with fabric. The only sewing that is needed is hemming. It's an easy and beautiful way to soften the top of a window. This French Provence fabric gives this kitchen personality and a decorating theme. The fabric is of a light weight so it was lined with a light yellow fabric. The owners wanted these lovely windows to remain uncovered, so this style of drapery is perfect in this case — it dresses the room but doesn't obscure the window view.

how to make a simple window scarf

supplies

Fabric (see step 3 for determining amount)
Brackets
Safety pins
Push pins
Yardstick
Ribbon or twill tape

instructions

1 Attach your brackets to the top of each side of the window frame or on the wall just outside the window frame.

2 Mark the center of the top of window frame with a light erasable pencil.

3 Place a ribbon or string in the brackets and allow it to swag to the length and width that you desire. Measure the length of the ribbon. Add in amounts for hems on each side of piece.

4 Cut fabric to this length. Hem all edges of the fabric.

5 Mark the center of your fabric with a safety pin. Also mark pleats every 3-1/2".

6 Gather up your fabric in pleats of approximately 3-1/2" each. Swags should have at least six or seven pleats.

7 While holding the folds in place, lay the fabric over the brackets. Line up the safety pin with the mark showing center of window. Remove the safety pin.

8 Pin the top of the swag on each side above the brackets with a pushpin or a small nail to keep the swag taut along the top.

9 Gently pull the center of the swag down at least 16 inches. ∿

Here is another easy treatment that only requires hemming of the fabric. Rubber bands secure the pouf that is held in place with decorative rings. This classic floral and cartouche design fabric is heavy cotton. No lining is required because the fabric is quite substantial and the backside shows very little from the outside. The style of the fabric coordinates beautifully with this formally decorated Georgian-style home. Because this is a stair landing, privacy is not an issue, and the outside light is needed to keep the stairs well lighted. This style is perfect for drapery that does not need to be closed.

simple
swag
and
pouf

how to make a simple swag and pouf

supplies

Fabric

Brackets or rings

Yardstick

Rubber bands

instructions

1 Attach rings or brackets to window frame as desired.

2 Measure your fabric for the desired finished length. Remember to allow for the amount you want to "puddle" on the floor. To determine the "pouf" amount, make a practice "pouf" with some fabric and secure it with a rubber band around the poufed fabric. Undo the pouf and measure it. Add this amount to your finished length. Hem all edges of fabric.

3 Pleat your length of fabric about every 3-1/2". (see "Simple Window Scarf" project for photo showing this procedure.) Hold or pin pleats in place.

4 Stretch the fabric tightly across the top of your window and tack in place. Keep pleats in place.

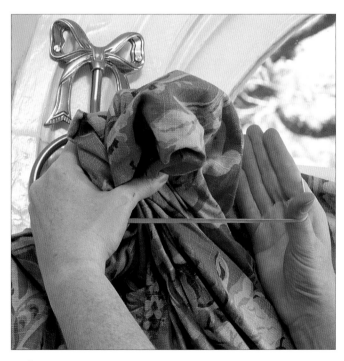

5 Make a pouf and secure it with a rubber band.

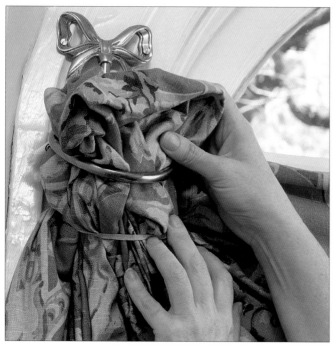

6 Pull the whole pouf in the rubber band through the ring.

8 If your pouf is flimsy or not to your liking, stuff it with tissue paper or net to give it more body.

7 Straighten and adjust the pouf as needed.

9 Pull the pouf out to make it pretty and puffy.∽

supplies

Pre-made window sheer (color to complement your room)

Metal drapery rod

Colored raffia or 1/4" ribbon (color to complement your sheer)

Pale violet acrylic glaze (or color a shade darker or lighter than your sheer for a tone-on-tone effect)

Rubber stamp of flower or other desired motif

Screw driver

Scissors

Disposable plastic plate (for palette)

magical swag

designed by Jeff McWilliams

instructions

1. Measure your window to determine the width of the sheer and the length of curtain rod needed. Purchase a pre-made window sheer and a curtain rod that will fit these measurements.

2. On a plastic plate, squeeze out some acrylic glaze. Paint the glaze onto the rubber stamp, covering the entire pattern on the stamp face. Stamp the pattern directly onto the sheer. This should be done on a firm surface which is protected with plastic bags or other protective cover under the sheer – the glaze will seep through the sheer fabric. Randomly cover the surface of the sheer with the stamp motif. Do not create any particular pattern with the motif placements.

3. Determine the top of your sheer. Gather sections of fabric unevenly in clusters along the top section (not just the top edge) of your sheer. The span of the clusters should measure from the top edge to one foot into the sheer. Once clusters are formed, tie the sections with one-foot lengths of raffia or ribbon. Refer to photo of project for guidance.

4. Install the metal curtain rod, using the instructions on the package. It should be attached beside the window frame, 1" from the edge of the window trim, and even with the top of the window.

5. Tie the raffia or ribbon to the curtain rod, alternating the bunches and allowing the curtain to remain at different heights. For the best look, change the order of bunches at one point to allow the sheer to double back along the rod.

versatile
panels

These great-looking panels are made of bed sheets, an inexpensive way to buy decorator fabric. The panels are made the same size as the window and attached to the window with loops that match hooks on the window frame. There are so many ways that these panels can be used. They can cover the entire window, they can cover half of the window, one corner can be raised — See 4 examples at the bottom of page 43.

how to make versatile panels

supplies

One twin bed sheet for center of panel
One twin bed sheet for border of panel
6 Cup hooks
Thread
Measuring tools
Scissors
Hand sewing needles
Sewing machine

instructions

1 Measure the inside of your window frame for the finished measurements of your panels.

2 Cut the center sheet fabric to the finished measurement minus 5" on each side for the border.

3 Cut eight 5-1/2" wide strips of fabric from the border sheet fabric. You should have four strips for the top and bottom that equal the finished width plus the seam allowances. You should also have four strips for the sides that equal the finished height plus the seam allowances.

4 With right sides together, sew the contrasting edge fabric to the center fabric, attaching long strips to long sides and short strips to short sides.

5 Sew the corners in a miter. Press all seams.

6 With right sides together, sew the additional matching border strips to the already sewn border strips (front) along outer edges.

7 Sew the corners in miter.

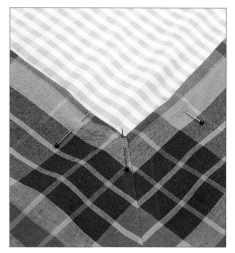
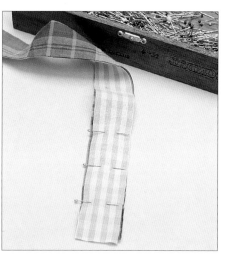

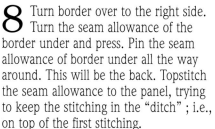

8 Turn border over to the right side. Turn the seam allowance of the border under and press. Pin the seam allowance of border under all the way around. This will be the back. Topstitch the seam allowance to the panel, trying to keep the stitching in the "ditch" ; i.e., on top of the first stitching.

9 Make six loops for attaching panel to cup hooks on window frame by cutting a narrow strip of each of the two fabrics and sewing each set together with right sides together. Leave a small opening for turning. Turn loops right side out and press. Sew opening closed. Cut loops to desired lengths and knot them at the ends.

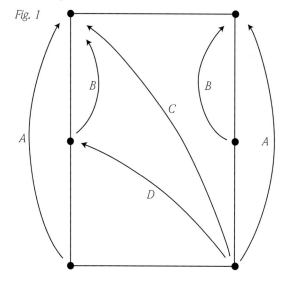

10 Hand sew the centers of loop strips to panels at the four corners at centers of each side piece. Hold panel up to window and mark window frame for positions of cup hooks. Secure cup hooks into window frame.

There are a number of ways these panels can adorn your windows. See Fig. 1 for ideas − then try some of your own. 1) The bottom corners could be folded up to attach at top corners as shown by arrows A. 2) The side loops could be folded up to attach to the top hooks as shown by arrows B. 3) One of the bottom corners could be attached at the diagonal top corner as shown by arrow C 4) One of the bottom corners could be attached at the diagonal side hook as shown by arrow D and in the photo above. ∾

Fig. 1

A B C B A D

43

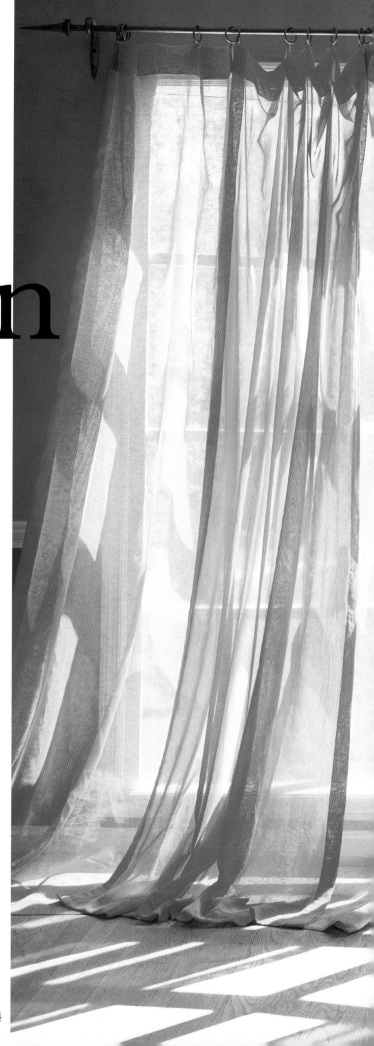

curtain
panels
with
rings

Straight panels are so easy to make. Yet when you choose a dramatic fabric and trendy hardware – they will definitely make a statement. Shown here, gauzy orange fabric in two different tones pud-dles on the floor and is mounted to the rods with sewn-on metal rings. The rod and brackets are wooden and have been sponged with gold metallic paint. The finials were handmade from mahogany by artist Roger Foster. The sponged orange walls match the color of the curtains. These curtains have a dramatic effect in daylight or night.

how to make panels on rings

supplies

Fabric for panels

Thread

Sewing machine

Rods and brackets

Rings

instructions

1 Cut fabric panels to size as determined by your window measurement. For this project, I used four panels – two each from different fabrics. The panels are not sewn together. To determine the amount of fabric, take the finished width measurement and multiply by two. Take the finished length measurement and add 6" for the top hem and 6" for the bottom hem (adding 12" total to the finished length measurement).

2 Turn under the sides of the panels 1/2" and press. Turn under another 1-1/2" and press again. Stitch down next to the inside folded edge.

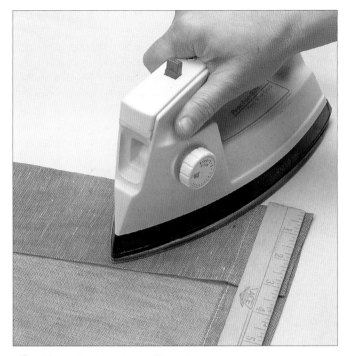

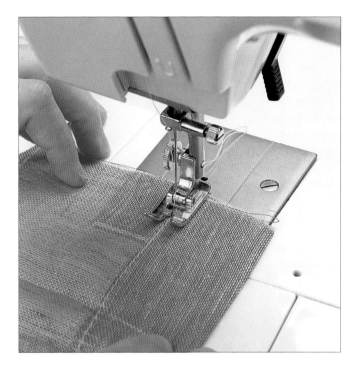

3 Turn the top down 3" and press. Turn down 3" again and press. Stitch next to the inside folded edge (Photo #3). Repeat this step for the bottom hem.

4 Sew metal rings onto the top edge of the panels. Slide rings onto the rod to mount curtain.

variation - gathered on the rod

This same style of curtain (using instructions 1 through 3) can be mounted by sliding it onto a rod, rather than using rings.

sheer
panels
with
tabs

These breezy panels add an air of drama to a contemporary decorated room. The neutral color scheme is not diminished by the sheer curtains – because they are almost transparent in the room – they simply soften and diffuse the light. The tabs at the top are made of a different fabric to add a special point of interest to the curtains. Mahogany rods and finials, handmade by Roger Foster, keep with the natural wood theme. Because the room is very stark and tailored, the soft puddling of the fabric on the floor creates an element of surprise.

supplies
Fabric for panels
Fabric for tabs
Thread
Sewing machine
Buttons

sheer
panels
with
tabs

how to make panels with tabs
instructions

1. Fold under the sides of panels 1-1/2" and press. Fold under again 1-1/2" and press. Stitch next to the inside fold.

2. Fold the top down 3" and press. Fold down again 3" and press. Stitch next to the inside fold. Repeat this step for bottom hem.

3. Make the tabs and hand stitch them to the tops of panels, gathering the ends of them in a small space. See instructions with simple steps below for making tabs.

4. Stitch a button onto bottom of each tab.

NOTE: You may do the whole process with fusible webbing or some other bonding material if you wish to avoid machine sewing all together.✎

how to make tabs

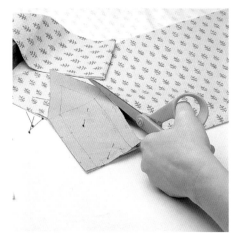

1 Cut double the number of tabs needed, following the tab pattern on page 28.

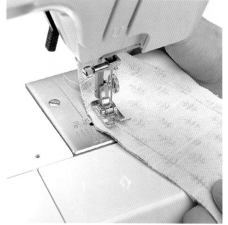

2 Put two tabs right sides together and stitch around the outside on the stitching lines. Leave the space between the dots unsewn to have an opening for turning.

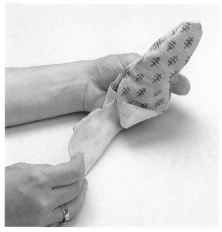

3 Turn tabs right side out through unsewn opening.

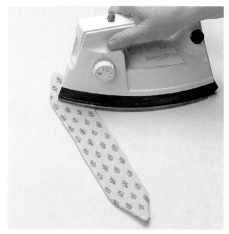

4 Press tab and hand sew opening shut **or** topstich the tab all the way around on the machine.

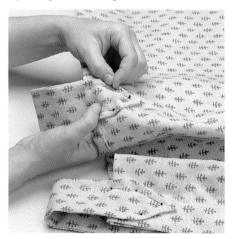

5 Pin the tab in place at top of finished curtain, pinning through the curtain and aligning the back of the tab with the front of the tab.

6 Stitch the tabs to the top of the finished curtain.✎

velvet
panels
on
rings

Soft, sensuous velvet is a favorite fabric for today's decorating. The fabric is durable, heavy, washable, and adds a regal quality to a room. These curtains can look formal or casual, depending upon the way they are mounted, the color, and the style of the room.

how to make velvet panels on rings

These panels are made the same way as "Sheer Panels with Tabs" (page 51). This style can be mounted in several different ways. The purple velvet panels have drapery hooks attached to the upper hem. The drapery hooks are then slipped into the eye rings of large wooden rings.

The moss green velvet panels shown in the photo on the following page are attached with clip-on metal rings (clipped directly to curtain) that slide over a thin metal rod.

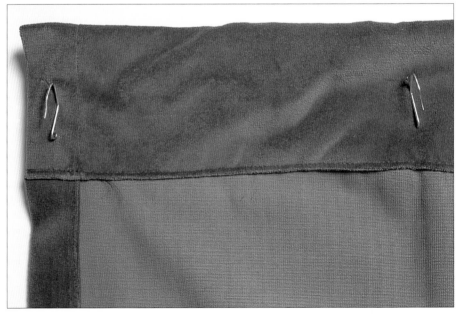

Cafe curtains cover only the bottom half of the window. Sometimes a valance is used as well at the top of the window for accent. These easy to make tab-top panels are given a more interesting homey flavor by sewing buttons randomly over them. Much more interesting than plain panels, the curtains bring life to a kitchen nook. Buttons can even be sewn onto purchased panels to create a custom look all your own. Curtains were designed by Anne McCloskey.

button bonanza
cafe curtains
designed by Anne McCloskey

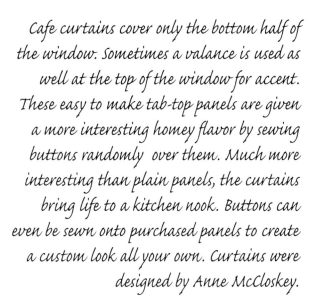

THE SANTA FE OPERA

THIRTY-NINTH SEASON
June 30 - August 26, 1995

how to make
button bonanza cafe curtains

supplies

Fabric for curtains and tabs
Large colorful buttons
Needle and thread
Scissors
Iron

instructions

1. Using your window measurements, determine the length of the fabric panels for your window. On the window shown, the top of the panels are flush with the center of the window – with the tabs being slightly above center. Cut fabric panels by your measurements, adding hem and header allowances. (Photo #1) The width of each of the panels is the width of the window (which would make the entire curtain two times the width). Sew panels together to make width for each panel if needed.

2. For the valance determine length desired. Our valance is the length of one of the window panes. Allow for bottom and top hem and cut fabric accordingly. The valance is only one panel that is double the width of the window. Sew panels together if needed to create proper width.

3. Hem the sides of each panel(Photo #2) and valance.

4. Hem top and bottom of each piece, panels and valance (Photo #3). Notice that the header is smaller than the bottom hem. If you wish to avoid machine sewing, hems can be ironed in place with fusible webbing (Photos #4 and #5).

5. Mark fabric for placement of tabs. Be sure that tabs are placed equal distances apart. The width of your curtains will determine the number of tabs needed. You will want to have one tab approximately every 6". (Photo #6).

6. Cut enough tabs using the pattern on page 28. Be sure to cut two tabs for each one tab needed.

7. Pin two tabs together, with right sides together and stitch, leaving an opening where shown on pattern for turning. Turn tab right side out and press flat. Sew opening closed.

8. Pin tabs to top of curtain. Center tabs on the marks made previously. Stitch in place. Hand sew a button at the point of each tab (Photo #7).

9. Hang on a colorful rod. A wood rod can be painted the color you desire (Photo #8).

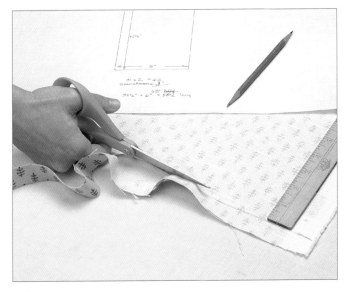

1

2

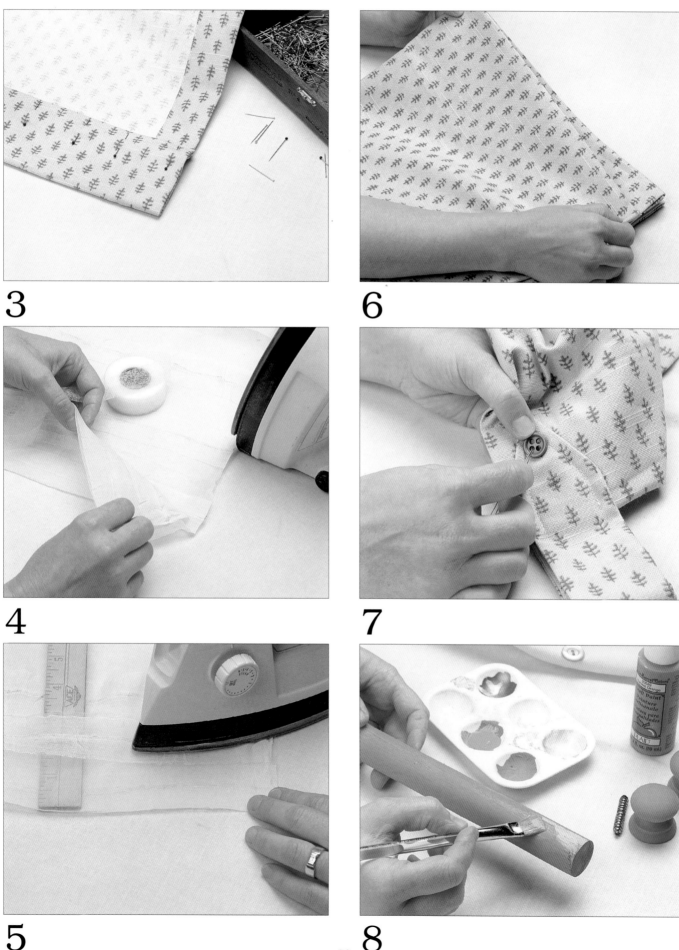

3

6

4

7

5

8

tea-towel
buttonhole
curtains

Tea towels make great curtains. They are already hemmed and ready to be fashioned to fit your windows. Here I used two different sets of antique tea-towels to make the panels, an embroidered set and a striped set. Large vertical buttonholes are made at the top of panels and the curtain rod threaded through them. These buttonholes can be decorative, if desired, as well as functional by stitching them with a contrasting color of thread. The same technique can be done with grommets, placing them where the button holes would be.

how to make
tea-towel buttonhole curtains

supplies

Tea towels or tea towel fabric
Border fabric
Thread (that contrasts with background color of curtain)
Wood rod, 1" diam.
Two drawer pulls with dowel screws (for ends of wood rod)
Spray paint for rod (color of trim and/or buttonhole thread)
Two brass coat hooks (for holding rod)

instructions

1. *For ready made tea towels,* measure your window to determine the number of towels you will need. *For tea towel fabric,* measure your window and cut fabric 2-1/2 times the width for fullness. Finish outer edges with colorful binding (See photo).

2. Make 2" long vertical buttonholes at top of curtain on your sewing machine, using contrasting thread (Fig. 1). Make buttonholes with a buttonhole attachment or zigzag machine stitch. For stronger or brighter buttonholes, stitch over the buttonhole a second time.

3. Paint a 1" wooden rod with color of trim and/or buttonhole stitching. Let dry.

4. Thread the rod in and out of the buttonholes (See photo).

5. Mount brass coat hooks to wall on each side of window. Hang rod on coat hooks.

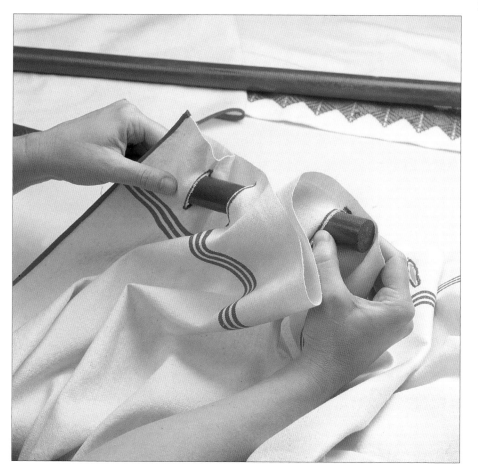

Fig. 1

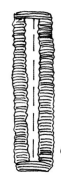

Cut on dotted line.

Sometimes, a touch of gathered fabric in the window is all that is needed. This treatment has an inside mount and the fabric is gathered at both top and bottom on a spring tension rod. It covers only the top third of the window and gives a very neat and tailored appearance. It is good for shortening the look of very tall windows, and is a perfect choice to combine with a stenciled border to dress up the window frame.

supplies
Fabric
Spring rods, 2 per window
Thread
Sewing machine

curtains
gathered on two rods

instructions

1. Cut fabric the desired length plus seam allowances. There is one panel per window. The width should be 2-1/2 times the finished width of the curtain. Sew panels together if needed to create the width needed.

2. Hem sides of panels with narrow 1/2" wide hems.

3. Turn under top and bottom edges 1-1/2" and press. Turn under again 1-1/2" and press. Stitch along inside fold, then stitch again 1/2" from edge at top and bottom to create casings. Adjust these measurements according to the diameter of rod you are using.

4. Thread a spring rod through each casing (at top and bottom) and place in window.

These purchased curtains have been decorated with a colorful stamped dragonfly design. There are a wide variety of stamps and block print designs available. Stamping is easy to do on fabric and can turn plain Jane curtains into a fashion statement. I layered the decorated shower curtain on top of the purchased tab curtains for a unique look. The teal ribbon attaches the shower curtain to the rod.

dragonfly
stamped curtain

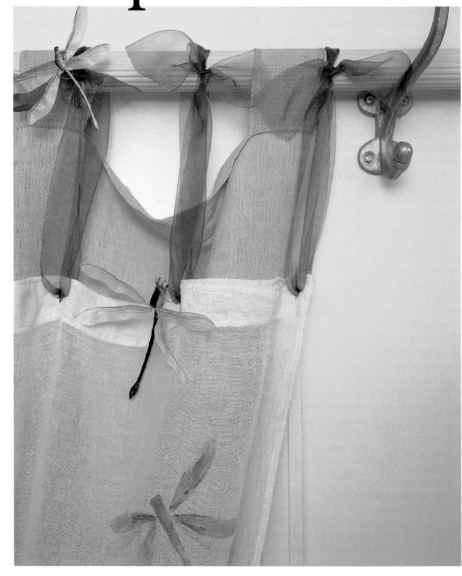

supplies

Purchased tab curtains
Purchased white gauze shower curtain
Teal ribbon
Three silk dragonflies
Fluted wooden rod
Wooden finials
Acrylic glaze:
    Blue-green
    Misty green
    Sunset yellow
Purchased dragonfly foam stamp or block printing design
Flat artist's brush and liner brush

instructions

1. Paint the body of the dragonfly block with blue-green (Photo #1).

2. Gently block print the body onto fabric (Photo #2).

3. Paint the wing block with misty green (Photo #3). Gently block print two wings on each side of body. Imperfections will not be noticeable when the whole pattern is completed.

4. Hand-paint the antennae with the yellow, using the liner brush.

5. Repeat wherever desired on front curtain.

6. Attach the silk dragonflies to the rod.

1

2

3

Make your own cornice board from wood or plastic foam or purchase a lightweight foam cornice board kit from a home supply store, or a fabric store. It comes complete with pre-cut pieces to fit most windows, brackets, pins, and adhesive. They are easy to cover with fabric – no sewing required. Here are simple instructions for putting them together.

cornices

supplies

Window Cornice Board Kit (includes liquid adhesive, trim pins, nails, and anchor tacks as well as cornice board parts)

Fabric:
Single Window – 64" long x 24" wide
Double Window – 100" long x 24" wide
(Dimensions include 1/2" all around for hem allowance.)

Scissors

Yardstick

Batting (Optional):
Single Window – 54" x 16"
Double Window – 90" x 16"

Utility knife (if crown needs to be shortened)

Iron-on fusible web or other iron-on bonding fabric (use to hem fabric instead of sewing)

instructions

To Assemble:

1. **Check your window size; you may need to shorten your cornice board.** If so, measure the amount you wish to cut off and, using a yardstick or ruler, make a line with pen or pencil on both sides of board. Score the board with light pressure, using a utility knife. Gradually increase pressure with each stroke. Repeat on other side of board. Edge will be covered with fabric, so it doesn't matter if cut edge is rough.

2. Assemble the two parts of the dust board and face board by applying a continuous line of adhesive to the center cuts of the dust board; join the two sections and apply pressure at both ends. Insert T-Pins to secure. Repeat with the face board. Let dry 8 hours.

3. Lay face board flat on the floor. Apply a generous amount of adhesive to the long, narrow edge of the dust board. Carefully place the adhesive edge of the dust board at top of the face board, forming a right angle. Press together firmly, making sure all surfaces are in contact and edges are straight.

4. Apply adhesive to one long edge and one short edge of one end board. Fit end board carefully into the right angle formed by face board and dust board. Be sure all surfaces are in contact and fit straight and evenly. Press firmly together. Let dry for 8 hours flat and undisturbed.

To Cover With Fabric:

1. Cut fabric and batting to size. Hem fabric to prevent fraying, with a sewing machine or use iron-on bonding web.

2. Lay cut piece of batting across face board and both end boards. (It is not necessary to cover dust board, which is usually not seen.) Allow 1" of batting to turn under the bottom edge of face board. Anchor corners, if desired, with fabric glue.

3. Lay face board down on backside of fabric.

4. At center of one end board, fold fabric to inside and secure with a trim pin. Insert pin at a 45-degree angle to board. Repeat at center of other end board. Pull fabric taut. Fold about 2" of fabric onto dust board at center and secure with

a trim pin. In the same manner, pull fabric to the inside of the bottom of face board at center and secure with a trim pin. These four pin positions establish the cross tension needed for a smooth, firm look. Complete attaching fabric to end boards, then dust board, and face board, by pinning the fabric every few inches, always pulling fabric taut. Miter fabric at corners.

5. There may be "extra" fabric when you reach the bottom corners of the end boards. Fold the fabric down while tucking under, then pin to the inside of the end board.

To Hang the Cornice:

1. Decide where you want to hang the cornice board, then determine where the brackets should be attached to the wall. The cornice board should be placed as high above the window as possible without the top of window frame showing. Brackets should be placed about 2" from each end of the cornice board.

2. Measure the correct distance above the window frame and mark the desired locations for brackets with a light pencil line. Make sure each line is level with the other.

3. Insert an anchor tack, sharp point up, through the small hole in the horizontal arm of the bracket. A drop of adhesive may be added at the base of the tack. Let it dry so that tack is secure in this position.

4. Brackets may be installed with nails and/or tape. If using nails, make a small mark on the wall through the two small holes in the bracket. CAUTION: If using tape, be sure measurements are accurate before removing the paper strip from the tape. Adjustments cannot be made after the tape is attached to the wall.

5. Rest the cornice board on the brackets. Use very gentle downward pressure to allow the anchor tacks to penetrate the board.∞

This cornice was covered with a fern print fabric and paired with metal bees for trim. To complete the theme, you can stamp ferns on sheer curtains with acrylic glaze or paint. Dimensions shown are 42" wide x 15" long x 6" deep.

supplies

Three coordinating fabrics:
Fern print fabric to cover the cornice, 1-1/2 yards of 54" wide fabric
Fabric for triangle interior, 1 yard of 54" wide fabric
Fabric for trim on triangles, 1 yard of 54" wide fabric
Cornice board kit
Polyester batting, 2 yards
Craft or utility knife
Pencil
Thread
Fabric scissors
Tape measure or ruler
Tailor's chalk
Sewing machine
Straight pins
Iron
Eleven decorative bees or other motif
Hot glue and glue gun

bee and fern
cornice

designed by Laney McClure

instructions

1. Assemble cornice board to fit your window, following instructions in kit.
2. Create a wave shape as shown in photo of project along the bottom front edge of the cornice by tracing the shape with pencil and cutting along the line with a craft or utility knife. The shape goes from 15" deep on the outer edges of the cornice to 12" deep at the center front.
3. Cover cornice board with batting, securing with T-pins.
4. Cover batting with the fabric chosen to cover the cornice, securing with T-pins. Set aside.
5. Cut the seven triangle pieces from fabric. The triangles measure 15-1/2" long and 12" wide, which allows for a 1/2" seam allowance on the top and sides and a 1" seam allowance on the point.
6. Cut strips of the triangle-border fabric that are 4" wide. Fold these in half length- wise and press with an iron.
7. Pin a border strip to each side of a triangle and sew strips and triangle together with a 1/2" seam allowance. At the point, create a mitered seam for the border strips. Turn under the unfinished end of the point and stitch down. Turn under the top edge of the triangle 1/2" and stitch. The overall finished dimensions of each triangle should be 18" long x 14" wide.
8. Pin the triangles to the flat top of cornice, overlapping them so that they evenly cover the front and sides.
9. Attach bees to the points of the triangles with hot glue as shown in photo of pro- ject.

This cornice is wonderful in a clubroom or den.
Dimensions for the cornice shown are 41" wide x 15"
long x 6" deep.

supplies

Fabric, 2 yards
Cornice board kit
Polyester batting, 2 yards
Nailhead trim
Craft or utility knife
Ruler
Pencil

tailored
cornice

designed by Laney McClure

instructions

1. Assemble cornice board to fit your window, following the instructions included in the kit.

2. Trace a scalloped shape along the bottom edge of the cornice, dividing the area into three equal sections. (Refer to photo of project.)

3. Cut out scallop shape by scoring the lines with a craft or utility knife, then gently breaking along the lines.

4. Cover the cornice with a layer of batting, using T-pins to secure along the back and edges.

5. Cover the batting layer with the fabric, securing with T-pins along the back and edges.

6. Attach nail head trim along the outer edges of the front and sides.

The ribbon and bows add a feminine touch. They also provide a unique area for displaying antique pins or other favorite similar items. Dimensions of cornice shown are 29" wide x 15" long x 6"deep.

supplies

Floral fabric, 1 yard
Wire-edged ribbon, 2 colors
Cornice board kit
Polyester batting, 1 yard
Decorative pins or other antique
    items to display on the ribbons
Craft or utility knife
Ruler
Pencil

cornice with
ribbon trim

designed by Laney McClure

instructions

1. Assemble cornice board to fit your window, following the instructions included in the kit.
2. Trace a scalloped shape along the bottom edge of the cornice, dividing the area into three equal sections. (Refer to photo of project.)
3. Cut out scalloped shape by scoring the lines with a craft or utility knife, then gently breaking along the lines.
4. Cover the cornice with a layer of batting using T-pins to secure along the back and edges.
5. Cover the batting layer with the floral fabric, securing with T-pins along the back and edges.
6. Using one of the ribbon colors, wrap ribbon vertically at a scallop indentation around the entire cornice and complete with a bow at the bottom. Repeat at other scallop indentation.
7. Using the other color ribbon, run lengths from the top of the cornice down to the front of the cornice and secure with T-pins. (See photo)
8. Attach decorations to the ribbons for display.

Big overlapping circles look like a cluster of giant buttons. This is a very unusual and interesting cornice. Dimensions of the cornice shown are 38" wide x 11" long x 3-1/2" deep.

supplies

Cornice board kit
Polyester batting, 2 yards
Four coordinating fabrics, 1 yard each
Neutral fabric to coordinate with the above fabrics
Cardboard
Covered button hardware, 3 sizes (1-1/2", 1", and 3/4")
Tassel, color to coordinate with fabrics
Scissors
Pencil
Ruler
Lightweight twine
Needle with oversized eye
Staples and stapler

button cornice

designed by Laney McClure

instructions

1. Assemble cornice board to fit your window, following the instructions in the kit.
2. Cover the cornice with the neutral fabric, securing with T-pins.
3. Cut cardboard templates for three sizes of circles: 12" (large), 8-1/2" (medium), and 6" (small). Three large, seven medium, and four small circles were used for the cornice pictured in the photo.
4. Cover each circle with batting, securing on the backside with staples.
5. Cover circles with the four coordinating fabrics, securing the fabric on the back with staples. Be sure that you lay the circles out first and choose which circles will have which fabric so that fabrics will look evenly spaced on the finished cornice.
6. Using the coordinating fabrics, cover the three sizes of covered button hardware.
7. To attach the buttons to the circles and the circles to the cornice, you will use one step: Using the large eye needle and lightweight twine, pierce all the way through the cornice face board coming from the backside of face board (inside cornice) and then through the center back of the circle. Run the needle through the back metal loop (shank) of the button and pierce back through the circle and cornice face board so that you have two ends of twine on the back of the cornice face board. Tighten the circle to the board by tying the twine ends together in a knot. For placement of circles, see photo of project.
8. When all circles are attached, hang the tassel on the large center circle.

Toile fabric and antique linens create a wonderful look for traditional décor. Take that lovely linen out of the attic trunk and place it where you can see and enjoy it – in the center of a window valence. Dimensions of the valence pictured are 53" wide x 20" long. If your window is a different width, make adjustments to the fabric dimensions given in these instructions.

supplies

Cornice board kit
Antique linens
Main fabric (toile), 2 yards of 54" wide fabric
Neutral fabric to coordinate with toile
Rope trim, 3 yards
Cotton thread
Button thread
Tape measure
Straight pins
Sewing machine
Fabric scissors

pleated valance
with antique linen

designed by Laney McClure

instructions

1. Assemble cornice board to fit your window, following the instructions in the kit.
2. Cover the cornice with the neutral fabric, securing with T-pins.
3. Cut the main fabric to 103" wide. If you use fabric that is 54" wide, you will need to cut two pieces and seam them together. The seam will be hidden in a box pleat. The length of the main fabric should be 18". These measurements allow for a 1/2" seam on all sides. Hem the toile valance fabric on both sides and the bottom. The seam allowance is 1/2".
4. Pin the toile fabric into pleats along the top of the fabric,

making box pleats as you pin. Each pleat has a 5" face and a 2" return. The area of main fabric that will hang behind the antique linen is not pleated. Press your box pleats well.

5. Pin the top of the pleated toile valance along the top of the cornice.

6. Pin a piece of antique linen to the center of the cornice.

7. Cut two pieces of the top border fabric, each measuring 4" wide x 54" long. Cut two 54" lengths of rope trim. Machine-sew the rope trim between the two (front and back) border fabric pieces along both long sides.

8. Pin the border piece along the top of the cornice. Be sure to hide the pins along where the rope trim is attached. ∞

No longer do we just think "curtains" when we think "windows." There are wonderful ways to decorate windows with painting. Shutters, shades, window boxes, and more can be what you need to decorate your windows – no frilly curtains for you. In this next chapter are lots of ideas for a variety of surfaces and techniques to use for painted window décor.

painted
window
decor

canvas

Canvas is a traditional surface that is durable and accepts paint well. It is easy to cut or fashion into a variety of sizes and shapes. It can be found at art or craft supply shops in pre-primed or unprimed form. Pre-primed is best – all you have to do is cut it to the correct size and begin painting.

wood

Plywood or thin birch wood is easy to cut and use for decorating a window. Many home workshops have band saws or zig saws that make it easy to cut creative wood shapes. After cutting the shape required, use an electric or hand sander to sand front and edges smooth. Seal with gesso or wood sealer, then sand again. You are now ready to paint the design.

supplies for painting

paints

Acrylic bottle paints are the best choice for decorative painting. You can find them at art and craft supply shops in a wide variety of pre-mixed colors. They are ready to use right from the bottle. Cleanup of brushes and spills is easy with soap and water while the paint is still wet.

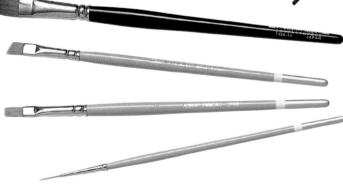

brushes

Good quality artist brushes are needed for decorative painting. Choose a variety of flat and round sizes. When painting an area, use the biggest brush to accommodate an area, using a minimum of brush strokes to fill in the area. Clean brushes after use and store in a jar, with the bristles up.

transferring patterns

For all decorative painted designs in this book, we have provided patterns to use for recreating the designs. If the patterns are not actual size, it is noted what size the pattern should be enlarged to make it full size. In most cases, the patterns can be enlarged on a copier. Trace the full-size pattern onto tracing paper. Position the tracing paper onto the surface you are going to paint. Tape the top or one side of the pattern in place. Slip a piece of graphite paper or transfer paper between the pattern and the surface. Retrace the pattern so that it transfers to your surface. Now you have a pattern of the design on your surface to help you paint in the design.

supplies

Artist's canvas, medium weight, pre-primed
Acrylic Paints:
    Light green
    Mustard yellow
Spray adhesive
Grommets and grommet tool
Ruler
Pencil
Dragonfly stamp
Sea sponge
1/2" foam brush
Cardboard (for diamond template)
Low-tack masking tape

canvas
dragonfly
valance

designed by Laney McClure

instructions

1. Cut a piece of canvas to fit the width of your window opening, adding 3/4" to each side for the side hems. Dimensions of valence pictured are 16" long x 50" wide.

2. Cut a diamond template from cardboard, so that when the rows of diamonds are traced onto the canvas, you end up with half diamonds on the outer edges. (Refer to photo of project.) The template used for the valence shown was 8-1/2" wide x 11" long. Lightly trace the template with a pencil onto the painted side of the canvas, being sure to account for the 3/4" hems.

3. Cut the bottom edge of the canvas along the lines of the diamond template so that you end up with a zigzag edge.

4. On the unpainted side of the canvas, apply spray adhesive to the edges and fold back 3/4" on each side to create the hems. Allow two hours to dry thoroughly.

how to stamp

1 Paint colors onto face of stamp with an artist's paint brush or foam brush.

2 Press stamp onto surface to be decorated. Lift stamp straight up.

5. To create the hang tabs, cut strips of canvas that are 2-1/2 " wide x 5" long. Spray the edges with adhesive and create 1/2" hems on the sides as you did in step 4. Allow to dry and set aside.

6. To paint the green diamonds, apply masking tape along the outer edges and paint inside the tape with light green paint; use the foam brush. (Refer to photo of project for placement.) Let dry. Repeat the same steps for painting the mustard yellow diamonds.

7. To paint the sponged diamonds, tape along the outer edges of some light green diamonds (refer to photo of project for placement) and sponge with the sea sponge over the existing light green paint with the mustard yellow paint. Let dry.

8. Stamp the dragonfly motif on the center row of light green diamonds using the dragonfly stamp and the mustard yellow paint. Apply paint to the stamp with the foam brush. Stamp the bottom row of mustard yellow diamonds using the dragonfly stamp turned upside down and light green paint. Let dry.

9. Paint the hang tabs with alternating light green and mustard yellow paints.

10. Attach hang tabs to the back of the canvas with grommets – two grommets per tab.

painted
garden
pots
shade

designed by Anne McCloskey

Pull this colorful shade down and it will brighten up your outlook. The scene is painted on a fabric window shade. If you can't find a high-quality canvas shade, buy an inexpensive vinyl one and replace the vinyl with canvas, using the old hardware. This is a clever way to cover an unsightly view or unattractive window.

painted garden pots shade

pictured on page 84

supplies

Purchased high-quality fabric window
  shade and findings
Acrylic paints:
  Black
  Dark brown
  Dark green
  Light blue
  Light brown
  Light yellow-green
  Medium green
  Medium purple
  Red-brown
  Rose
  Sky blue
  Turquoise
  White
  Yellow
  Yellow-orange
Purchased flower pot stencils or cut
  your own
Black permanent medium-point marker
Pencil
Sea sponge
Kitchen sponges
Clip clothespins
Gloss acrylic sealer
Clear acrylic glazing medium
Brushes:
  Medium round tip
  Small square tip
  1" foam brush
Optional: Stencil material blank and
  utility knife if cutting your own sten-
  cils

instructions

Paint directly on the fabric shade or replace a vinyl shade with canvas.

1. **Background:** Mix glazing medium and light blue paint together. Using sea sponge, sponge in the background from top to about three-fourths of the way down, using a circular motion to create the sky. With the same technique, sponge white paint in clumps to resemble clouds, creating an overall cloud pattern. Go over the clouds several times so that clouds stand out. With the foam brush, paint a yellow-green + glaze mix on the bottom portion of the shade. Let dry.

2. Transfer the pot and trunk shapes to the canvas or cut your own stencils of these shapes.

3. **Topiary (right):** Using a small amount of paint, sponge in the sky blue pot, sponging in the open area of stencil. Paint in the turquoise rim at top. With the round brush, paint simple squiggle lines in a random pattern on the pot. Stencil the trunk with dark brown, using the sea sponge. Highlight it on the right side with red-brown. Trace around a paper plate at the top of the trunk for topiary ball. With brush, basecoat the topiary circle with light yellow-green. Squeeze out three shades of green paint. One at a time, sponge medium to dark green shades over the circle to form the foliage. Dab a little white over the foliage ball in places for accent. Water down the medium green and smear around the topiary circle. Make sure the circle overlaps the tree trunk at the bottom. Smear a watered down red-brown along both sides of the trunk. Dab dark brown in top of pot to look like soil. Dab light yellow-green and medium green to simulate moss on top of the soil in topiary pot, overhanging the pot. Water down the medium green. Stroke from topiary moss outward to look like spiky leaves.

4. **Foliage pot (center):** Stencil dark brown center pot. While wet, sponge white over it in places to create a rounded look. Let some of the brown blend with the white. Cut leaf shapes from kitchen sponges and dampen them. Paint dark green paint onto the sponge leaf shapes and press above pot in a curved pattern, beginning about 6" above the pot. Turn the leaves so that they are facing different directions. Start at the top and form a curved row. Fill in until the leaves overlap the top of the pot. Outline the veins with strokes of light yellow-green. Paint a watered down medium green around outer leaves.

5. **Pot of violets (left):** Stencil the red-brown pot. Sponge white over the wet paint as you did before. Sponge medium green leaves, using the same sponge leaf shapes. Double load the small flat brush with purple and white paint. Stroke in five-petal violets among the foliage. Vary the sizes. Buds are single petals. Create a wash around the leaves as you did with the previous pot.

6. With red and dark brown, paint a light shadow around the bottom of the pots. With a medium green wash, paint grass blade strokes around the pots.

7. **Butterfly:** Transfer the butterfly pattern above the center pot. With the flat brush, outline and paint in the top portion with yellow and the bottom with yellow-orange. Paint left and right sides in a splotchy manner with turquoise. Create a semi-circular shape with rose and add a black circle in the center. Dab white in the middle of the circle. Paint a red-brown splotch at bottom of each wing with a white circle and a black center. Paint the butterfly's body and head with purple; add a stroke of yellow-orange. Paint antennae with purple. Paint circles around the top with black with white dabs. When dry, outline the butterfly and around the large splotchy shapes with the marker.

8. When dry, replace slat in casing and hang your new shade.☙

Topiary Tree Trunk Full-size Stencil Pattern

←   *extend to 10"*

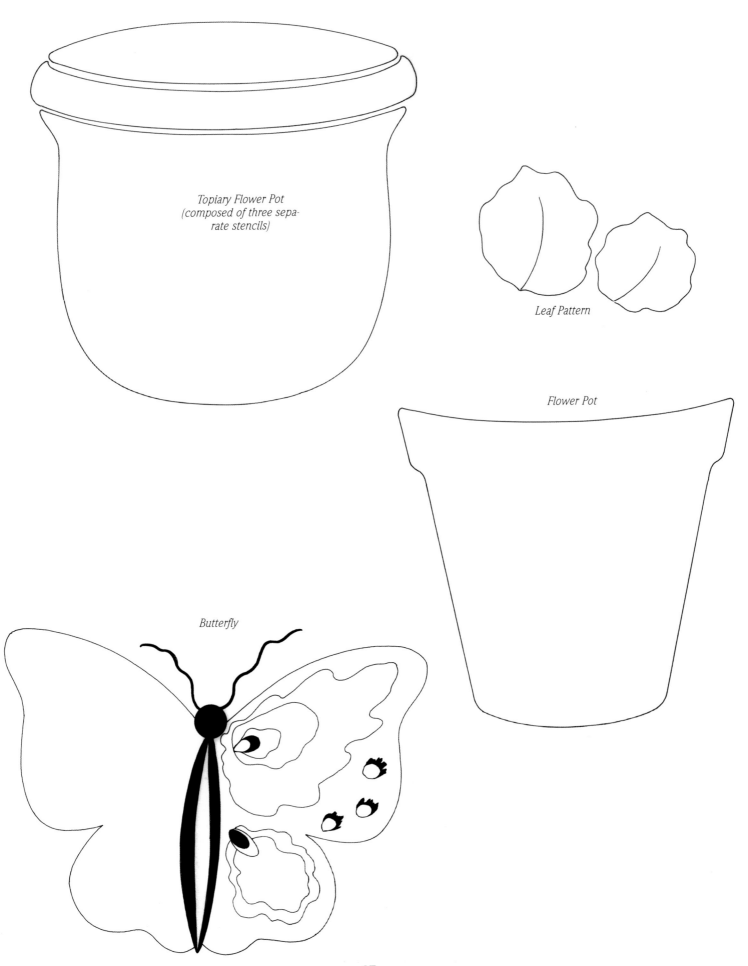

Topiary Flower Pot
(composed of three separate stencils)

Leaf Pattern

Flower Pot

Butterfly

robins & branches
window shade

designed by Susan Dumas

supplies

Window shade (best quality)
Prints for birds and leaves
Decoupage medium
Semi-gloss indoor/outdoor paint: dark
 blue, white
Acrylic paint: burnt umber, white
Sponge brush
Stencil brushes, medium and small
Craft or utility knife
Optional: Stencil material blank

instructions

1. Mix a little dark blue paint into the white paint to make the light blue sky color. Apply two or three coats to the window shade. Let dry completely.
2. If making stencils for the tree branch, trace pattern of branch onto stencil blank and cut out with a craft or utility knife. If painting rather than stenciling, transfer pattern to shade.
3. Stencil or paint the branch with burnt umber + white (a beige mix). Go over the first layer with burnt umber, letting a little of the light color show through. Apply white paint to just the upper part of the branches for highlighted areas.
4. Cut out bird and leaves from prints. Apply to the shade with a thin coat of decoupage finish. Refer to photo of project for positioning.
5. Paint clouds with white paint and the stencil brush, using a circular motion. Then smudge the wet paint with a paper towel or cloth to create a "cloud" texture.

Branch: enlarge @200%.
Transfer with graphite paper or trace on
stencil blank material and cut a stencil.

birdhouse shutters

designed by Anne McCloskey

supplies

Roll of pre-primed artist canvas or pre-cut wood

Canvas grippers

Staple gun and staples

Wooden canvas stretcher strips: Four 14" and four 36" (this makes 2 panels)

Scissors

Birdhouse stencils (or stencil material blank and craft or utility knife for cutting stencils)

Acrylic paints:

  Black

  Dark brown

  Dark green

  Ivory

  Light blue

  Light green

  Medium green

  Orange

  Purple

  Sky blue

  White

  Yellow

  Yellow-orange

Gloss acrylic glaze sealer

Gesso

Brushes:

  Foam brush

  Medium flat brush

  Small round brush

Sea sponge

Pencils

Screw eyes

Picture wire

Graphite paper

Instructions follow on page 92

birdhouse shutters

pictured on page 90-91

supplies listed on page 90

instructions

1. **Assemble shutters:** Assemble stretcher strips to form two shutter panels. Cut canvas 4" longer on all sides than the stretcher strip frame. Lay out canvas with white (pre-primed) side down. Place stretcher strip frame on top of canvas. Using grippers, grip canvas while pulling it, starting in the center of the long stretcher, and staple. Turn the stretcher around, pull, and staple to the same place on the opposite side of frame. Now, pull and staple each end in the center. Go back to where you began and continue stapling each side until the canvas is very taut .Tuck and pleat the raw edges at the corners, and staple to the inside of stretchers so that corners lie fairly flat. Complete the other panel the same way.

2. Water down a portion of gesso in a bowl and apply with a foam brush to coat each panel including the sides. This will remove any lingering wrinkles. Line up both panels so you can work on them side by side while painting, almost as one unit.

3. **Sky:** With foam brush, paint three-fourths of the way down from top of panel with sky blue paint. Blend in light blue closer to the top of panel to lighten it. With sea sponge, swirl in clouds with white paint using a circular motion. Create an all-over pattern with clouds, but keep them softly blended into sky. (Ground will be painted later.) Do the same on the other panel with the sky and ground (to be painted later) meeting in the same place.

4. **Cut Stencils:** Transfer the patterns of birdhouses, birdhouse holes, and poles to stenciling material. Cut the stencils with a craft or utility knife. Refer to photo of project for positioning birdhouses. Make sure the one birdhouse is lower than the other one for interest on the panel with two birdhouses. Place the birdhouse on the other panel in the center a little lower than the taller one on the panel with two birdhouses.

5. **Birdhouse #1:** Stencil this birdhouse with rose paint, using the sponge. With a hint of black on the sponge, lightly dab shadows on both sides. Position the stencil for birdhouse holes and stencil with white, using the sponge. Sponge black over the left portion of each hole. Apply black to the roof with a white line underneath. Center the pole under the birdhouse and sponge-stencil with black. Make sure the pole is long enough to be sitting in the portion that will be the grassy area. Apply black to the bottom rectangle (base of birdhouse).

6. **Birdhouse #2:** Sponge-stencil the birdhouse with

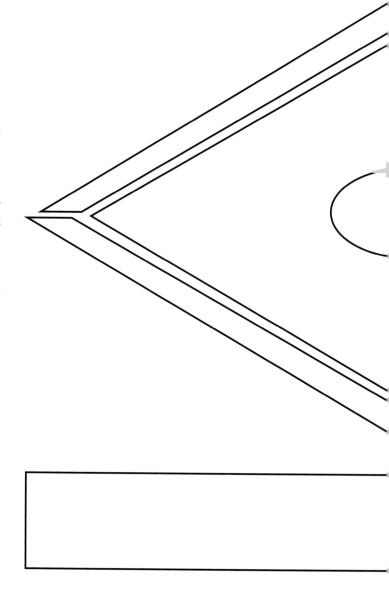

medium pink. Lightly sponge over it with rose to shadow it. Sponge-stencil the hole with white; then sponge black over the white except in highlight area as before. Sponge-stencil the roof with black with a white line underneath. Stencil the pole the same as the previous one.

7. **Birdhouse #3:** Sponge-stencil with purple to shadow it on both sides. Create the holes, roof, and pole the same as the other birdhouses.

8. **Grass:** Create the grass by painting on a medium green background, using a foam brush. With watered down light green, lightly stroke out blades of grass over the bottom of the poles, and into where the sky meets the ground. Stroke in the three shades of green, one at a time, curving and overlapping each grass blade.

9. **Five-petal Flowers:** Double load purple and white onto a flat brush and stroke it to the flower center to

Additional patterns on page 94

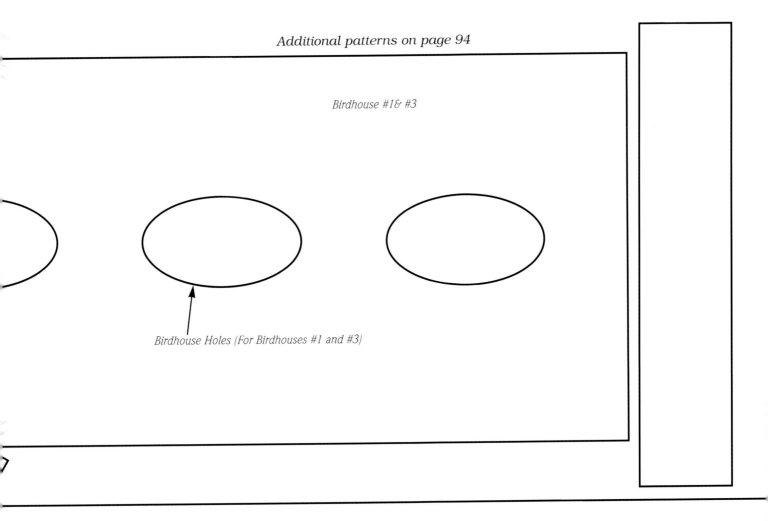

Birdhouse #1& #3

Birdhouse Holes (For Birdhouses #1 and #3)

Birdhouse Pole (extend and vary heights of poles) ───────────────►

create a petal. As you do this, slightly squiggle the brush creating an irregular, rounded petal. Paint five petals for one flower. With tip of brush dab in a yellow-orange center with a little yellow at top. Create short strokes of black around center, and lightly dab a little black in center. The buds are one elongated stroke of purple and white. Paint light green stems. Sprinkle the flowers around bases of birdhouses. The larger cosmos flowers should come closer to the foreground. Paint grass and flowers at the same level on both shutters so that they will match up when installed.

10. **Daisies:** With round brush, stroke approximately nine long white petals to the center to form a daisy. Blend white and black to form a gray; softly stroke on inside of each petal. Dot yellow in center, dab gray around edges, and dot black in center. Make buds with white dots with light green stems.

11. **Bird:** With graphite paper, transfer the bird pattern to canvas so that it is perched on the top right of the sin-

gle birdhouse. Paint the entire bird shape with yellow-orange; let dry. Transfer the wings, chest, eyes, head, and beak. Paint the top of head with black, using round brush. Dot the eye white. Paint the wing with black, stroking in white to outline areas and blending it in. Paint the chest with orange and blend white into it. Drybrush a little black around the chest edges. Stroke yellow around the wings on the main body. Drybrush black to shadow the main body. Paint beak with orange with a hint of white on the lower beak. Drybrush black around beak to define it.

12. Paint the sides of the panels blue and green to match the painting.

13. When dry, smoothly apply one or two coats of glaze sealer to panel fronts and sides. Since these are shutters, the two panels should be hung in the same way. Twist in screw eyes and picture wire about 6" from the top of the panel back and hang on each side of window.∽

birdhouse shutters patterns

instructions on page 90-93

Bird

*Blue flowers
(enlarge and reduce to
vary size)*

Birdhouse #2

*Birdhouse Hole (For
Birdhouse #2)*

*Daisy
(enlarge and reduce to vary size)*

The birdhouse shutters look great combined with a picket fence installed in the lower half of the window with ivy or other vine attached to the picket fence and up one side and across the top of the window as if growing there.

picket fence

designed by Susan E. Mickey

supplies

Ten wood grade stakes, 1" x 2" x 36"
Two wood laths, 1" x 2" x 12"
Medium grit sandpaper
Paint brush, 2"
White high gloss acrylic paint
White finishing nails, 3/4"
Four 2" hinges
Front closure such as latch

instructions

1. Determine the number of grade stakes needed to fit the size window you wish to cover. Divide this number by two in order to have two panels which open in the middle. Window treatment shown has five 2" grade stakes with 1/2" spaces between them to fit a 24" wide window. Cut the two 12" laths into four equal lengths to attach to the top and bottom back of the grade stakes.
2. Sand all pieces; wipe clean of dust. Paint pieces with two or three coats of high gloss white acrylic paint.
3. Mark the grade stakes where you want to nail the lath cross sections on the back. On the window treatment shown, laths are 5" from the top and bottom. Nail the first and last grade stake to the top lath, then go back and add the grade stakes between, measuring each space between for consistency. Repeat with second lath at the bottom. (It may be necessary to touch up these laths with a further light coat of paint after nailing them in place.)
4. Attach the hinges and front closure to "fence" and install picket fence to the window frame.

A wooden cutout is attached to a planter box to create "faux" flowers that bloom in any season.

geranium
window box

designed by Anne McCloskey

supplies

One large sheet of 1/4" thick ply-
 wood
Plastic, wood, or clay planter box, 16"
 to 20"
Gesso
Acrylic paints:
 Dark brown
 Dark green
 Dark rose
 Fuchsia
 Ivory
 Light green
 Light pink
 Medium green
 Medium pink

Red-brown
Tan
White
Gloss acrylic sealer
Brushes:
 Foam brush
 Medium round brush
Flat sponge cut into three
 shapes – rectangle, leaf,
 and petal (patterns on
 page 99)
Fine grit sandpaper
Ruler
Pencil
Silicone glue

Instructions follow on page 98

geranium window box

pictured on page 97   *supplies listed on page 96*

instructions

1. Prime the inside and the outside of the planter with gesso.
2. Paint the outside and the tucked fabric inside with dark brown paint.
3. Squeeze out small puddles of medium brown, red-brown, ivory, and tan paints onto a plastic plate. Cut a 1" x 3" rectangle from a flat sponge and dampen it. Randomly paint three or four colors at a time onto the sponge, placing ivory in the center. Begin pressing the first horizontal rectangle at the bottom left. Allow a small space next to it and then press the next rectangle. Complete the row. For the second row you will stagger the rectangles so that they will overlap the open spaces, creating a basketweave look. Continue in this manner for all rows. With tan paint, create a border stripe under the top row. Finish the front including any overhanging areas.
4. When dry, apply one or two coats of sealer.
5. Make the wooden geranium panel: Trace the pattern onto plywood. Cut out, sand edges and surfaces, and remove dust with tack cloth.
6. Paint the front, back, and sides with dark green.
7. Using patterns, cut a leaf shape and a petal shape from the sponge. Dampen sponge shapes.
8. Squeeze out white and three green paint shades. Blend the colors onto the leaf sponge.
9. Starting at the bottom left, press the sponge onto the wood. Do the same to the next sponge but turn the sponge in another direction. Repeat the process until you have completed a row. Leave some space in between the leaves so that the dark green background shows through. Complete the rows until the entire shape is filled with leaves.
10. The one petal shape sponge will create the flower clusters. Squeeze out fuchsia, medium pink, dark rose, and white paint . This time dip the sponge into the paint so that it will be applied thickly. Dip sponge into each color and press petals into clusters. Allow some of the green background to show through petals. Make some of the clusters larger than others, and make some small ones to resemble buds. Sponge some flowers darker than others for contrast. Keep the design open so that leaves show through.
11. Double load the round brush with light and medium green, and stroke on stems that gently curve. Dot a ball of light green at base of buds for calyxes.
12. Touch up any leaf areas with dark green where you need the accent.
13. When dry, apply one or two coats of glaze.
14. Place the geranium panel into the box. Use silicone glue to attach it to the inside of the planter. Or support it from behind, insert a heavy object.∽

patterns

Rectangle for Basketweave
Cut from flat sponge

Leaf Shape
Cut from flat sponge

Petal Shape
Cut from flat sponge

Geranium Panel
(half pattern – place on fold)
Cut from plywood

Enlarge pattern at 183%

folk art
window kitty

designed by Anne McCloskey

supplies

Laminated pine boards, 1" x 8" x 36" and
  1" x 10" x 36" (see Step 1 for sizes to
  cut)
Acrylic paint:
  Black
  Clay
  Dark brown
  Dark yellow
  Ivory
  Red-brown
  White
  Yellow-orange
Brushes:
  Foam brush
  Small and medium round brushes
  Flat brush
Vises
Wood glue
Tracing paper
Fine grit sandpaper
Black medium tip permanent marker
Pencil
Ruler
Sea sponge
Gloss acrylic sealer

instructions

1. Measure, cut, and assemble all parts to insure proper fit. Cut a 4" x 11" back, a 5" x 9-5/8" bottom, two 4" x 5-1/2" sides, and one cat shape according to pattern (it is 7-1/8" x 13-3/4"). With wood glue and vises, glue the back and sides to box bottom. Keep the vises on until the pieces are securely affixed. Center and glue the cat shape to the front, aligning bottoms. Lightly sand and remove any dust.

2. Apply a coat of sealer to inside and outside the box; let dry.

3. Paint an undercoat of dark yellow paint, using foam brush, to the same areas; let dry.

4. Trace the cat pattern onto tracing paper. Place the tracing over the cat shape and transfer pattern on cat with a pencil, outlining the main sections.

5. **Cat Face:** With a round brush, paint red-brown on top and sides of head. Stroke on stripes of yellow-orange and brown. Paint nose with brown and add an ivory accent. Outline ears with red- brown. Lightly sponge inside ears, around mouth, chin, sides of nose, cheeks, and above eyes with brown. Dab over cheeks with tip of a flat brush, and stroke around chin and mouth with dark brown. Lightly stroke over nose, around mouth, and on chin with ivory. Paint eyes with white. Add black circles for pupils. Dab one large and one small white dot in each eye to highlight them. When face is dry, outline eyes, eyebrows, ears, cheeks, nose, mouth, striped areas, and around head with the marker. Also use the marker to draw whiskers and whisker dots around mouth.

6. **Cat Body:** Outline legs, haunches, tail, and spots with the marker. With a flat brush, paint a dark brown scallop shape at the top of each spot. Around that, paint another scallop with red-brown, then a scallop with clay. Use the same technique on the leg in the center of the cat. On the leg at the left, sponge on dark brown and red-brown. Under the head, sponge yellows and browns with more dark brown at the sides. Sponge the haunch or thigh area with a dark brown outline, then softly sponge with red-brown. Sponge dark yellow on the inside of the remaining spot. Paint in a red-brown scalloped shape with dark brown inside. Outline tail with stripes of dark brown and red-brown. Sponge bottom of tail with dark brown. To accent the body, lightly sponge ivory on the areas that you have just completed. Paint two curved lines with red-brown under the head to simulate wrinkles; dry.

7. Sponge dark brown on the sides, back, insides, and bottom of box.

8. When dry, brush on the glaze sealer on the inside and outside of box.

Folk Art Window Kitty
Enlarge pattern @200%

rustic window frame

designed by Laney McClure

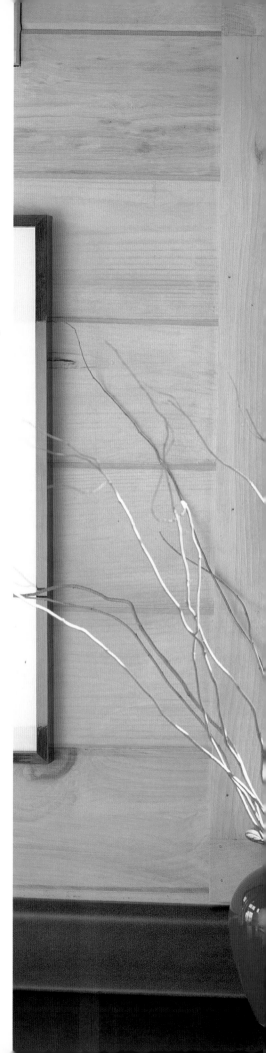

Instructions follow on page 105

rustic window frame

pictured on page 103   supplies listed on page 105

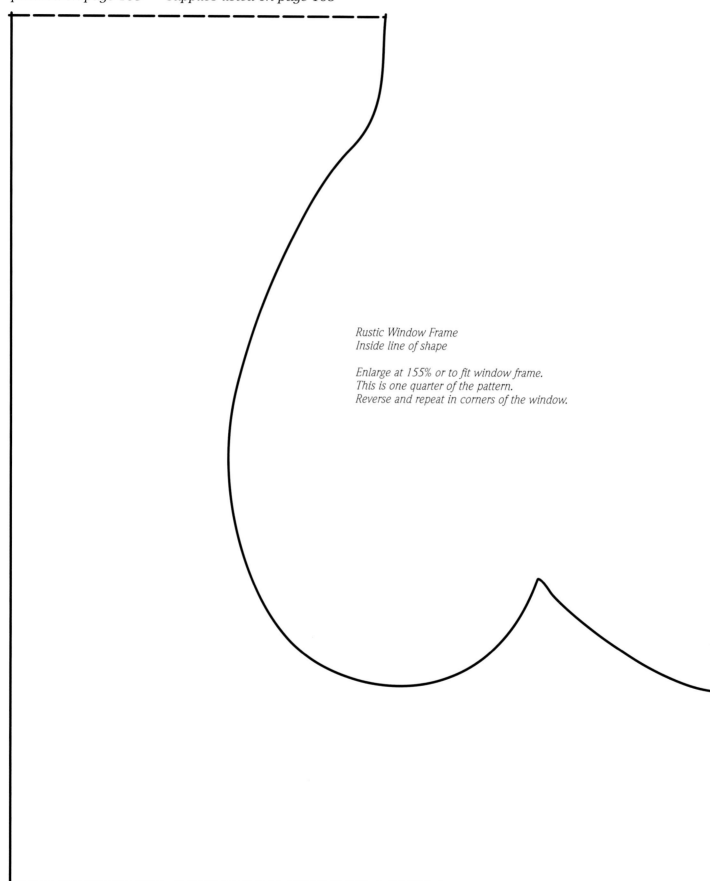

Rustic Window Frame
Inside line of shape

Enlarge at 155% or to fit window frame.
This is one quarter of the pattern.
Reverse and repeat in corners of the window.

supplies

White 1/4" thick plywood
Acrylic paints:
   Light green
   Moss green
   Mustard yellow
   Off white
   Tan
Gesso
Brushes:
   1-1/2" foam brush
   1/4" stencil brushes (one for each
   color in the flowers)
Floral stencil of your choice
Craft or utility knife
Pencil
Ruler
Tracing paper and stylus
Matte acrylic spray sealer

instructions

1. Cut the piece of plywood to fit the inside dimensions of your window.
2. Transfer the pattern provided onto the wood.
3. Cut the wood along the transferred lines.
4. Seal the wood with gesso, sand.
5. Basecoat the frame with two coats of tan, using the foam brush.
6. Stencil your selected floral pattern around the frame, using the stencil brushes. Use off white, moss green, and mustard yellow for the flowers and light green for the stems or vines. Let dry for several hours.
7. Finish with two light coats of matte acrylic sealer.∾

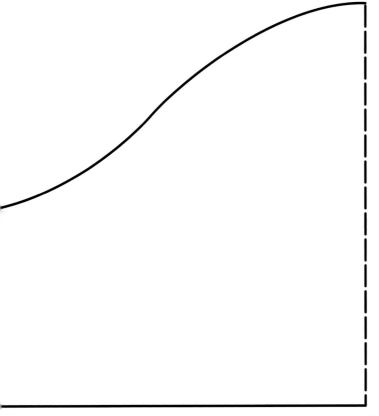

Windows can look like the high art stained glass windows done by masters. Today it can be done without the tedious work by using faux glass stain paint. An entire window, a border, or any portion of the window can have the stained glass look. Modern products make it easy.

painted
faux
stained
glass

glass stain supplies

Liquid Leading comes in a squeeze bottle. Squeeze it along the design lines, following a pattern, and it dries to look like real leading.

Glass Stain Paint in a variety of colors can be squeezed from the bottle tip into the leaded sections of a design for the look of authentic stained glass, even on vertical surfaces.

Leading Blanks are plastic sheets onto which you can do a whole design or a motif – the leading, then the coloring. Whey dry, peel it up and press it in place onto the window. It's self adhesive! Leading strips can also be made on leading blanks, let dry, then cut to the lengths needed and pressed into place on the window.

What's more, if you ever change your mind about your window treatment or change to a decor it no longer fits, simply peel it all off!

*Pictured right: "Hearts Times Four"
Instructions follow on page 108*

This design, with the motif positioned in the four corners of the window, can accommodate a window of almost any size and shape.

hearts
times four

designed by Laura Brunson

supplies

Faux glass stain paint:
 Amber
 Crystal
 Emerald
 Ivy
 Rose
 White pearl
Leading blanks
Liquid faux leading

(This design used with permission from Plaid Enterprises, Inc.)

instructions

1. Trace the pattern from book. With traced pattern under the leading blank, lead the four heart motifs. Make two with the pattern face up. Reverse the pattern for the other two, so that you will have two that are mirror images of the other two. Let leading dry.

2. Add glass stain paint in the leaded sections, referring to pattern for colors. Let dry.

3. Make extra straight leading lines on a leading blank for border. Let leading dry. Place ready-made leading on window for border. You may vary the width of border to fit window.

4. Add glass stain paint to borders, referring to pattern for colors. Let dry.

5. Peel up heart motifs and position one in each corner of window with points at corners of borders (refer to photo of project).

6. After placing the hearts, connect them to the borders with extra leading strips, cutting them to fit.

7. Paint the background between hearts and borders with clear glass stain paint.

8. The remainder of the window can be painted with crystal or left unpainted.◦◦

Color Key

R = Rose

E = Emerald

C = Crystal

I = Ivy

R = Rose

WP = White Pearl

A = Amber

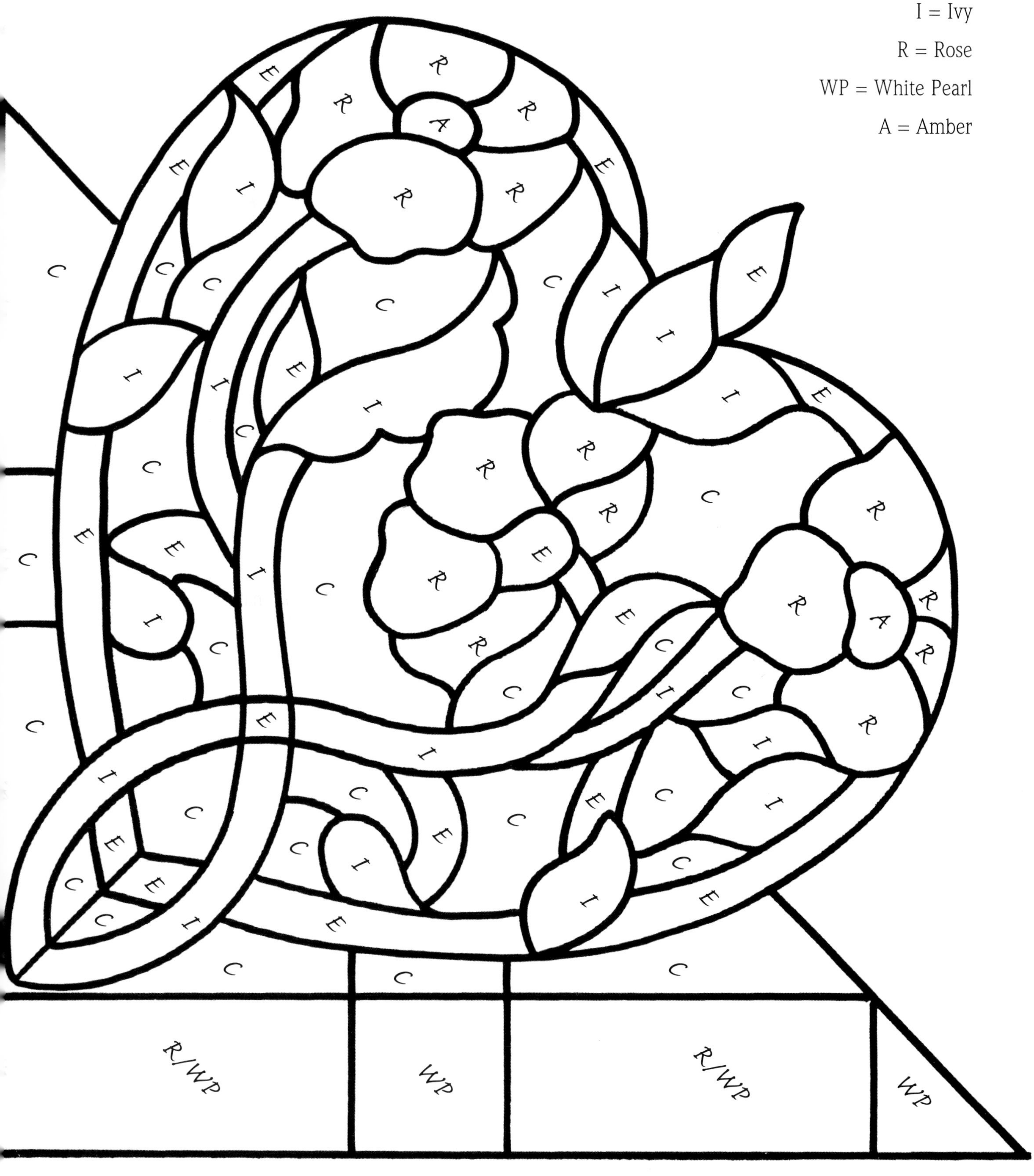

planted
blooms

designed by Laura Brunson

supplies

Faux glass stain paint:
  Amethyst
  Black
  Cocoa
  Kelly Green
  Orange
  Ruby
  White
  Yellow
Leading blanks
Liquid faux leading

instructions

1. Trace the pattern from book. With traced patterns under the leading blanks, lead the flower pots and flowers. Flowers can be used singly, in pairs, or as a group. Let dry.

2. Add glass stain paint in the leaded sections of pots and flowers, referring to patterns for colors (or use colors which coordinate with your decor). Let dry.

3. Peel up the designs and adhere to window across bottom.∞

Patterns follow on page 112

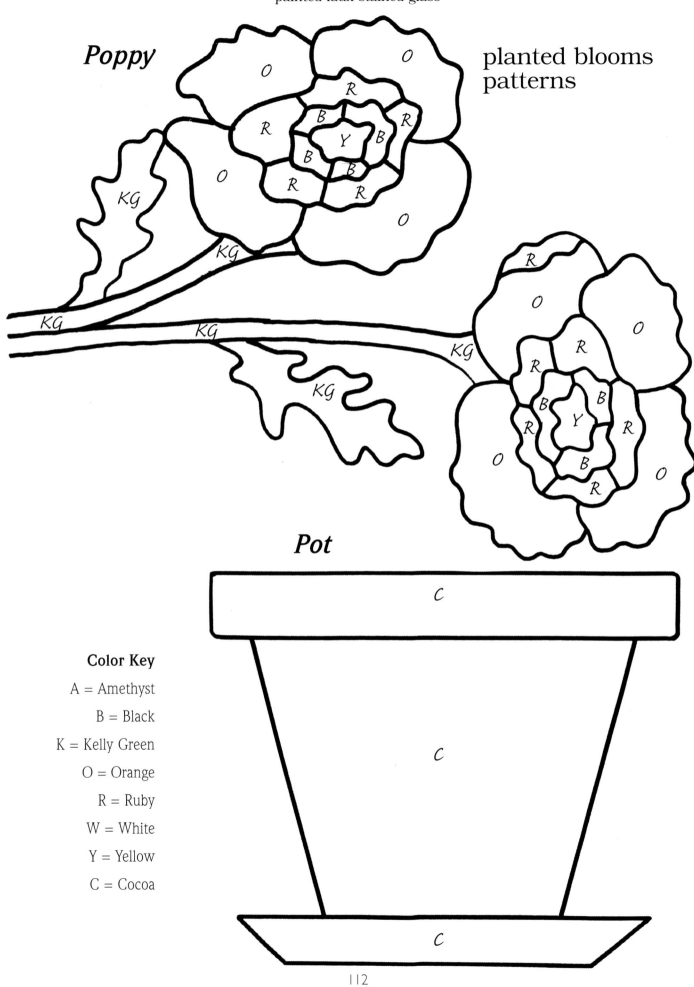

Poppy

planted blooms
patterns

Pot

Color Key

A = Amethyst

B = Black

K = Kelly Green

O = Orange

R = Ruby

W = White

Y = Yellow

C = Cocoa

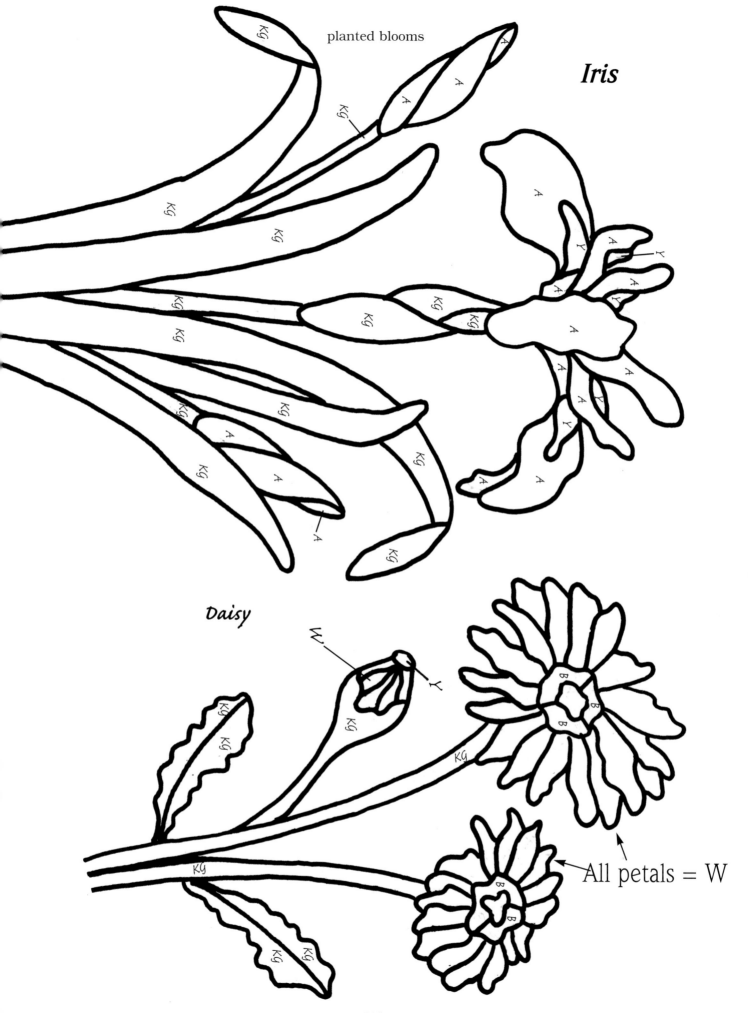

planted blooms

Iris

Daisy

All petals = W

113

Decorative architectural treatments can also be used in windows, and they can be made from very simple materials. In past times, lattice was often used in this manner. Today there are a host of other ideas and easy ways to use them. Scroll shapes can be cut from foam core board, painted, glued to an L bracket, and installed in window corners (with or without curtains). A fancy-shaped plywood border can be cut, painted, and installed in the window. Branches can be laced together for window blinds. Wood chicken cutouts and chicken wire can decorate a cornice. Think dimensional. Think one-of-a-kind. Think inexpensive. Think ingenious!

architectural
window decor
corner interest

designed by Laney McClure

Interesting brackets are available at home décor supply stores. You can find them finished or unfinished. Add them to the corners of your windows for a special look.

supplies

Decorative wood L bracket
Acrylic paints:
   Brick red
   Black
   Metallic gold
Sea sponge
Craft or utility knife
Thick white glue
Matte acrylic spray sealer

instructions

1. Basecoat the wood bracket with brick red. Sponge with black and metallic gold. When dry, spray with matte acrylic sealer.
2. Attach the wood bracket in one corner of window.

A cornice is cut from plywood to create this country theme design. Kitchen towels are attached to a rod with ring clips for the bottom café-style curtains.

roosting chickens
cornice & curtains

designed by Jeff McWilliams

supplies

Birch plywood, 1/2" thick (amount
   depends on window size)
Fine gauge chicken wire
Acrylic paints
   Brick Red
   Bright blue
   Mustard
   White
   Yellow
Medium grit sandpaper
Antiquing medium
Wood glue
Staple gun and staples
Metal "L" brackets, 2"
Screws
Screw driver
Hammer
#4 finishing nails
Jig saw or power saw
Hobby saw
Metal adjustable curtain rod
Two standard kitchen hand towels
One pkg. metal clip rings for drapes

instructions

1. Measure the width of window outside of window frame. Using this measurement plus 2", layout the front section of the cornice. This includes 1" for the thickness of the 1/2" plywood and 1" for extra space. The height of the panel is 12". Cut the front panel from plywood with the jig saw or power saw.
2. Cut two 12" x 4" side panels from the plywood.
3. Cut the top from plywood, the width of the front panel x 4-1/2". This measurement includes the side panels plus the thickness of the front panel.
4. Assemble the wood cornice board with wood glue and #4 finishing nails. Let glue dry.
5. Sand rough edges and wipe clean. Paint the entire surface with white acrylic paint. Let dry.
6. Stain the painted cornice board with brown acrylic paint. Apply and wipe off excess with a rag. This will allow some white to show through.
7. Using patterns provided, cut 11 plywood chickens, using the jig saw or hobby saw.
8. Paint the chickens with acrylic paint, referring to photo of project for colors. Let dry.
9. Sand the edges of the painted chickens.
10. Glue chickens to the front of the cornice board with wood glue. This works best if the cornice board is left flat until glue is dry.
11. Cut a section of chicken wire that will completely cover the surface and wrap it around the edges of the wood cornice. Tack the wire firmly in place with a staple gun.
12. Hang the cornice with metal L brackets attached to the window trim 1" from the outside of the trim and even with the top of the window.
13. Attach metal curtain rod halfway down window, using the hanging clips from the package.
14. Using ring clips attached to the top edges of the kitchen towels, hang two kitchen towels onto the curtain rod.

roosting chickens cornice & curtains

instructions on page 116

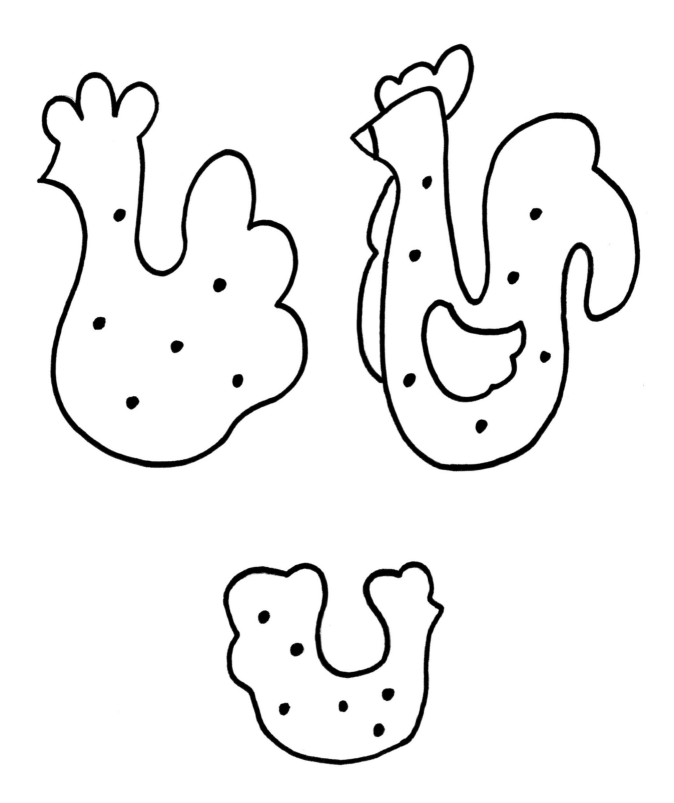

Make a place for your pottery, and create a window treatment at the same time, with a shelf at the top of your window. This idea works well in a kitchen and also in a back entry-way to your house or on a porch. It allows you and your guest to enjoy your collection.

the upper shelf

designed by Jeff McWilliams

supplies

Pre-built wooden shelf to fit your window
  width (from local hardware or craft store)
Semi gloss white paint
Medium grade sandpaper
White country crocks
Drywall hanging bolts
Two sawtooth hangers
Hammer
Screw driver

instructions

1. Measure window, and purchase shelf to fit. Make sure the shelf will clear the window trim on each side. Select a shelf closest to the exact size of your window. If an appropriate shelf is not available, see "How to Build a Shelf" instructions which follow.
2. Sand entire surface and wipe off dust.
3. Paint shelf with two coats of semi-gloss white paint; let dry after each coat before proceeding.
4. Attach sawtooth hangers to back of shelf.
5. Attach shelf to the wall with drywall hanging bolts and screwdriver. Make sure it is attached securely; it will hold pottery.
6. Place pots on shelf.

---

how to build a shelf

supplies

Shelving board cut to size of
  window opening (including
  the side window trim)
Two wooden shelf brackets

instructions

1. Determine length of shelf (from outside edge of window trim to outside edge of window trim on other side). Select shelving board this length or have it cut to this length..
2. Assemble shelf brackets and shelving board for a custom sized shelf.

supplies

Sticks (birch, beech, or ash tree branches work best)
Leather 1/4" lacing (available on a roll at your local craft or fabric store)
Two drapery pole holders
Screws
Screw driver
Measuring tape

twigs
at the window

designed by Jeff McWilliams

instructions

1. Measure window from molding to molding to determine length of your sticks (width of window treatment). Locate and harvest the tree branches. The branches can be different shapes and diameter. This will create the uneven pattern in your finished "blinds." Trim off any small limbs and twigs on each branch, leaving only the branch itself.

2. On a flat surface (the floor works well), lay out the branches side by side in the order you want them to be arranged for your blinds. Make sure that all the fatter ends do not end up on the same side. Allow for variations in the shapes of the branches. This layout is to verify that you have enough branches to cover half to three-fourths of your window, depending on how much of the window you still want to see through.

3. Cut leather strapping into four sections. The length of each strap should be three times longer than the length of your final window treatment. For example, if you want to cover one foot of window, the straps should measure three feet long.

4. Tie a knot with two of the leather straps for one side; tie a knot with the other two straps for other side. Place the knots at the top branch 3" in from each end, with one strap of each set in front and one in back.

5. Loop the leather straps around the top branch and tie a knot with the two straps below the branch. Do this on each side with each set of straps. Repeat this with the second branch, then continue in this manner to attach the remainder of the branches until you have your desired length. Tie a final knot with each set of straps at the bottom.

6. Attach the drapery pole holders 2" from each side of the window trim at the top of the window frame. Rest the top branch in the holders. Holders should be approximately 2" from the ends of the branch and well out of the way of the leather strapping.

This is a great use of birdhouses. Brightly colored houses can be used to tie the colors of any room together. Closeout Christmas ornaments make great birdhouses.

birds
on a branch

designed by Jeff McWilliams

supplies

Sticks (birch, beech, or ash tree branches work best)

Cup hooks

Variety of pre-finished small birdhouses (9 used in project shown); a variety of types for greater interest – metal, rough wood, natural, and others

Picture frame wire

Drywall screws

Screw driver

instructions

1. Measure your window width to determine the length branches needed. Locate and harvest the tree branches of varying lengths and thicknesses.
2. Cut off any leaves and the smallest parts of the branches, leaving only the parts of each branch that can support the small birdhouses.
3. Referring to the photo of project, arrange the branches over the window. Don't let all branches go in the same direction. Intertwine branches for best results.
4. Attach the branches to the window trim above and around the window with drywall screws. Make sure the branches are securely fastened to the trim to allow for the weight of the branches and birdhouses.
5. Most birdhouses need a cup hook to hang by. Simply screw the cup hook into the top of the house and they are ready to hang. Using the picture wire, wrap birdhouses into place at various levels on the branches. Some of the houses can be secured by screwing the cup hooks into the bottom of the house for perching them on the top side of a branch.

Vintage Linens folded and hung on a wooden fluted rod make a nice "collage" valence. These linens can change out seasonally and can also be beautiful in bright colors and patterns.

easy ideas

These blue glass bottles let the light
through and create colorful patterns on
the floor and walls. Use any combina-
tion of colors and heights.

supplies

Various textures and colors of art paper
Spray adhesive
Scissors
Binder clips
Picture hanging wire
Screw eyes (2)

handmade
paper shade

designed by Laney McClure

instructions

1. Cut a piece of art paper to fit your window. This will be the background paper for the whole design. Dimensions shown are 25" wide x 37" long.

2. Cut out shapes from the other colored papers to create a collage. Before gluing them to the background paper, lay them out to make sure that you like the pattern you have created.

3. Attach the papers by lightly spraying the backs with spray adhesive. When all papers are applied, allow to dry for a few hours.

4. To hang the curtain, put screw eyes into the wall on each side of the window opening. String picture wire between them, and attach paper to wire with the binder clips.

metric conversion chart

Inches	MM	CM		Yards	Meters
1/8	3	.3		1/8	.11
1/4	6	.6		1/4	.23
3/8	10	1.0		3/8	.34
1/2	13	1.3		1/2	.46
5/8	16	1.6		5/8	.57
3/4	19	1.9		3/4	.69
7/8	22	2.2		7/8	.80
1	25	2.5		1	.91
1-1/4	32	3.2		2	1.83
1-1/2	38	3.8		3	2.74
1-3/4	44	4.4		4	3.66
2	51	5.1		5	4.57
3	76	7.6		6	5.49
4	102	10.2		7	6.40
5	127	12.7		8	7.32
6	152	15.2		9	8.23
7	178	17.8		10	9.14
8	203	20.3			
9	229	22.9			
10	254	25.4			
11	279	27.9			
12	305	30.5